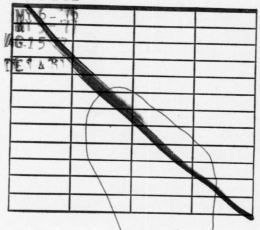

APPELLATE COURTS

IN THE UNITED STATES AND ENGLAND

The Judicial Administration Series

This series is published under the auspices of the National Conference of Judicial Councils. The purpose of these books is to help to promote a better, more efficient judicial system; to improve the present and advise as to the future, by presenting pertinent, timely discussions of important subjects, based on researching the past and offering concrete suggestions as to future improvements in our judicial system.

The nine books which now make up the series are:

*1939   *Lester B. Orfield:* Criminal Appeals in America

*1940   *Roscoe Pound:* Organization of Courts

1941   *Roscoe Pound:* Appellate Procedure in Civil Cases (*Oceana Publications, Inc., $7.50*)

*1942   *George Warren:* Traffic Courts

*1944   *Evan Haynes:* The Selection and Tenure of Judges

1947   *Lester B. Orfield:* Criminal Procedure from Arrest to Appeal (*Oceana Publications, Inc., $5.50*)

1949   *Arthur T. Vanderbilt:* Minimum Standards of Judicial Administration (*Oceana Publications, Inc., $7.50*)

1952   *Robert Wyness Millar:* Civil Procedure of the Trial Court in Historical Perspective (*Oceana Publications, Inc., $7.50*)

1963   *Delmar Karlen:* Appellate Courts in the United States and England (*New York University Press, $6.00*)

* Out of print.

APPELLATE COURTS

IN

THE UNITED STATES

AND ENGLAND

DELMAR KARLEN

FOREWORDS BY

LORD EVERSHED

AND

WILLIAM J. BRENNAN, JR.

1963

New York University Press

ACKNOWLEDGMENTS

The following chapters of this book have appeared in substance in the following periodicals:

Chapter 2   17 *Record of the Association of the Bar of the City of New York* 535 (December 1962)

Chapter 3   34 *New York State Bar Journal* 315 (October 1962)

Chapter 4   17 *Record of the Association of the Bar of the City of New York* 500 (November 1962)

Chapter 5   11 *International and Comparative Law Quarterly* 976 (October 1962)

Chapter 6   72 *Yale Law Journal* 266 (December 1962)

Chapter 7   48 *American Bar Association Journal* 1128 (December 1962)

Chapter 8   46 *Journal of the American Judicature Society* 126 (December 1962)

Chapter 10   78 *Law Quarterly Review* 371 (July 1962)

To the publishers of these periodicals, the author wishes to express his appreciation for their permission to reprint.

TO

SIR GEORGE COLDSTREAM

whose titles of "Permanent Secretary to the
Lord Chancellor" and "Clerk of the Crown
in Chancery" obscure the central and vital
role that he plays in the administration of
British justice.

CONTENTS

FOREWORD

By William J. Brennan, Jr.

ASSOCIATE JUSTICE, UNITED STATES SUPREME COURT

This promises to be a book of lasting significance. It is an attempt
to convey to the bench and bar generally the insights gained by
a handful of English and American judges and lawyers in a recent
comparative study of appellate courts in the two nations. An
American team observed appeals in the English courts in London
during July of 1961. An English team observed appeals in selected
state and federal courts in this country in January of 1962. The
members of both teams spent many hours in both countries in
discussions with one another and with court personnel and lawyers, appraising and criticizing what they saw. Each team gave
particular consideration to whether adoption of some of the features of the other nation's system might be desirable and feasible.
Professor Karlen, who was one of the members of the American
team, supplemented his participation in these discussions and
observations by three months of further intensive on-the-spot
study of the English system.

The main body of the book consists of a series of detailed
descriptions of the tribunals observed. It provides an inside view
of how these courts operate and contains much information
which has never appeared in print before. Apart from their obvious value to appellate advocates, these chapters may have an

even more profound value in the contribution they make to a better understanding of the essential nature of the appellate process.

The final chapter compares the general pattern of appellate procedure in England with that found in the United States. It reveals more contrasts than similarities between the two systems, and in so doing provides a stimulus for reflection as to what improvements might be made in each system. While it is apparent that neither country would, could, or should substitute the other's system for its own, there are features in each system worthy of serious consideration by judges and lawyers of the other nation. The long-range effect of stimulating such thinking is presently incalculable, though it is bound to be substantial.

As one of the few persons privileged to participate directly in the project out of which this book arose, I am delighted to see its benefits disseminated widely through this publication.

By Lord Evershed

HOUSE OF LORDS (FORMER MASTER OF THE ROLLS)

I am proud to have been invited, with my opposite "team captain" Mr. Justice Brennan, to write a foreword to this book; and, like him, I commend it as a work of lasting significance and add, to his, my own sincere appreciation of the great work done by its author.

It is, I take it, axiomatic that the welfare and survival of a free community depend upon its having a system of law which has the confidence of its members. The system known as that of the English Common Law has been adopted by a third of the world's population, living in free communities, of which England and the United States are two. But when we speak of a "system of law" we are apt to think too much of substantive law and far too little of the way in which in fact the law operates. Yet for the ordinary citizen—and for the maintenance of his trust in the law— the method may be more significant than the substance. And, to my mind, added emphasis is given to this view by the fact that in the present age all the free states of the world must legislate considerably upon every aspect of the ordinary citizen's life.

These considerations, if well founded, add enormously to the importance of the subject matter upon which the two teams of English and American lawyers devoted their energies and to which this book is dedicated. One result has been to make us in England reflect critically upon our own appellate methods, and the experiments so far tried show, at least, what, within the framework of our system, may be done for the benefit of the system and of the litigant whose position in the system plainly demands the highest consideration.

I

AMERICAN APPEALS

CHAPTER ONE

INTRODUCTION

This book grew out of a unique experiment in Anglo-American legal study, recently concluded. In essence, it was an investigation by English jurists of American appeals and by American jurists of English appeals. The goal was to discover the strengths and weaknesses of both systems, with a view to each nation considering such improvements in its own methods as might be suggested by insights gained from the study.

The American Visit to England

In July of 1961, an American team went to London for two weeks of observation and discussion of the English way of handling appeals. It consisted of the following persons:

William J. Brennan, Jr., Associate Justice of the United States Supreme Court

Charles S. Desmond, Chief Judge of the New York Court of Appeals

J. Edward Lumbard, Chief Judge of the United States Court of Appeals, Second Circuit

Walter V. Schaefer, Chief Justice of the Illinois Supreme Court

Archibald Cox, Solicitor General of the United States

Stanley J. Mosk, Attorney General of California

Delmar Karlen, Professor of Law, New York University and Associate Director (now Director) of the Institute of Judicial Administration

The American team was received by an English team consisting of the following persons:

Lord Evershed, Master of the Rolls (since appointed a Lord of Appeal in Ordinary)

Lord Morris of Borth-y-Gest, a Lord of Appeal in Ordinary

Sir Kenneth Diplock, a Judge of the Queen's Bench Division of the High Court (since elevated to the Court of Appeal as Lord Justice Diplock)

Sir Seymour Karminski, a Judge of the Probate, Divorce, and Admiralty Division of the High Court

Sir George Coldstream, Permanent Secretary to the Lord Chancellor and Clerk of the Crown in Chancery

Frederick W. Beney, Queen's Counsel

Richard Butler, Member of the firm of Charles Russell & Co., Solicitors

Arthur Goodhart, Master of University College, Oxford, and Editor of the *Law Quarterly Review*

Norman Marsh, Director of the British Institute of Comparative & International Law

The English team briefed the American team, mostly by detailed oral expositions of English appellate practice. It was assisted from time to time by other judges, barristers, and solicitors, who participated in some of the discussions. Among them were: Lord Justice Patrick Devlin, a member of the Court of Appeal (now a Lord of Appeal in Ordinary); Lord Justice Edward Holroyd Pearce, a member of the Court of Appeal (now a Lord of Appeal in Ordinary); Sir Reginald Manningham-Buller, Attorney General (now the Lord Chancellor); Lord Merriman, President of the Probate, Divorce, and Admiralty Division of the High Court (now deceased); Master Adams, Chief Taxing Master, Supreme Court; Mr. Boggis-Rolfe, of the Lord Chancellor's Office; Mr. R. P. Cave, of the Judicial Office of the House of Lords; Mr. Peter Foster, Queen's Counsel; Mr. Gerald Gardiner, Queen's Counsel and former Chairman of the General Council of the Bar; Mr. Griffith-Jones, Senior Prosecuting Counsel in the Central Criminal Court; Master King, Senior Master of the Court of Criminal Appeal; Mr. Randall Lane of the British Council; Mr. Geoffrey Lawrence, Queen's Counsel and Chairman of the General Council of the Bar; Sir Bertram Long, Senior Registrar of the Probate, Divorce, and Admiralty Division of the High Court; Sir Thomas Lund, Secretary of the Law Society; R. E. Megarry, Queen's Counsel, assistant editor of the *Law Quarterly Review,* and member of the Law Reform Committee; and Mr. Registrar Wyman, Chief Chancery Registrar.

Members of the American team observed in operation the Court of Appeal, the Court of Criminal Appeal, the House of Lords, and the Divisional Court of the Probate, Divorce, and Admiralty Division. They did so under ideal conditions, for they were assisted at every stage by the judges and clerks of the courts involved. They had ample opportunity to discuss the operations of those courts and the cases being heard not only with those officials but also independently with counsel involved in the cases. At the time of the visit, the Divisional Court of the Queen's Bench Division and the Privy Council were not sitting, but their operations were described and explained to the American team.

The English Visit to the United States

In January of 1962, the English team, now somewhat altered in composition, paid a return visit to the United States. Lord Denning, then a Lord of Appeal in Ordinary, but since made Master of the Rolls, took the place of Lord Evershed and Lord Morris of Borth-y-Gest; Sir Jocelyn Simon, then Solicitor General of England but since elevated to the Presidency of the Probate, Divorce, and Admiralty Division of the High Court, took the place of Mr. Beney as the barrister member; and Sir Dingwall Bateson, past President of the Law Society, took the place of Mr. Butler as the solicitor member. Otherwise the members of the team were the same persons who had received the Americans in London the previous July.

Because appellate courts in the United States are numerous, diverse in operation, and geographically dispersed, and because distances between them are great, the return visit had to be carried out along somewhat different lines than the London visit. A manageable but representative sampling of courts had to be chosen. It consisted of the following, each of which was observed in operation by the English team: the United States Supreme Court, the United States Court of Appeals for the Second Circuit, the New York Court of Appeals, and the Appellate Division, First Department, of the New York Supreme Court.

The briefing of the English team was done mostly through written papers, describing the courts to be visited and explaining specialized aspects of American appellate procedure. Thus there were papers on law clerks, rehearings, and like topics. Some, but not all, were written by members of the American team. Oral briefings of the kind held in London were generally not feasible, chiefly because of the geographical dispersion of members of the American team. Individually, however, they participated in conversations with their British counterparts and helped to make the necessary arrangements for other discussions and for observations.

Among others who helped the English visitors in their inquiries, special mention should be made of the Honorable Bernard Botein, Presiding Justice of the Appellate Division, First Department, of the New York Supreme Court, and his colleagues, the associate justices of that court. They, no less than the judges of the courts directly represented on the American team, helped to give the English visitors an intimate insight into appellate practice in the United States. Also deserving of special mention are: Associate Justice Tom Clark of the United States Supreme Court; Judges Charles E. Clark and Henry J. Friendly, both of the United States Court of Appeals for the Second Circuit; Chief Justice Frank Kenison of the Supreme Court of New Hampshire; Professor Norman Dorsen of the School of Law of New York University; Professor Shelden D. Elliott of New York University Law School and former Director of the Institute of Judicial Administration; Professor Howard Greenburger of the School of Law of New York University; Philip Heymann, Esq., of the Office of the Solicitor General of the United States; Professor Harry Jones of the Law School of Columbia University (now Research Director of the American Bar Foundation); Professor Robert A. Leflar, of the Law School of the University of Arkansas and Director of the Institute of Judicial Administration's Seminar for Appellate Judges; Louis Loeb, Esq., former President of the Association of the Bar of the City of New York and a trustee of the Walter E. Meyer Research Institute of Law; Orison Marden, Esq., President of the Association of the Bar of the City of New York; Lewis Mayers, Esq., Professor Emeritus of the College of the City of New York; Professor Gerhard O. W. Mueller, of the School of Law of New York University; Dean Russell D. Niles, of the School of Law of New York University; Professor Robert Pasley, of the School of Law of Cornell University; Professor Francis Sullivan, of the Law School of Loyola University (Chicago); Whitney North Seymour, Esq., President of the American Bar Foundation and former President of the American Bar Association and of the Association of the Bar of the City of New York; and Dean William Warren of the Law School of Columbia University.

Mutual Criticisms

On the last day of the visit in the United States, a meeting was held between the English and American teams. It was decided that each man should reduce to writing his individual critical observations of the other system. These would be "intramural" documents, intended only for the eyes of the members of the two teams, and would be a first step toward ascertaining what changes in domestic procedure, if any, ought to be recommended by each team. It was recognized on both sides that there could be no crude borrowings by either nation from the other, but that the ultimate value of the interchange of visits would lie in the critical introspection engendered by them.

These papers were duly prepared, exchanged, summarized,

and considered. They form a foundation for future study and for possible action in each nation.

Follow-up

In the spring of 1962, the academic member of the American team returned to London with the goal of reducing to writing some of the insights derived from the interchange. This book is the result. It is intended to spread the benefits of the study beyond the relatively few people who directly participated. Among the many persons who furnished advice, information, and assistance on this final phase of the operation, special mention should be made not only of the members of the British team, but also of Lord Parker of Waddington, the Lord Chief Justice of England, and Sir Thomas Ashworth, a Justice of the Queen's Bench Division of the High Court.

Results in England

In England, action looking toward improvement in appellate procedure is already under way. In the spring of 1962, the Court of Appeal inaugurated an experiment designed to reduce the amount of time spent in reading by counsel in open court during the course of argument. That was one of the focal points of discussion between members of the two teams. The experiment, which is described in Chapter 6, has resulted in an alteration in British practice.

At about the same time, the Divisional Court of the Probate, Divorce, and Admiralty Division altered its practice, again partially in response to the stimulus provided by the interchange. The changes, which are described in Chapter 9, involve advance reading by the judges of the record on appeal and the assumption of greater responsibility by them for putting their decisions into shape for publication in the *Law Reports*. These also were matters discussed between members of the two teams.

But the force of the project is not spent. Fundamental issues have been raised and fundamental thinking stimulated, which may have long-range, though presently unpredictable, results.

Results in the United States

In the United States, changes will come more slowly, partly because there are 51 separate systems rather than one to deal with, partly because American procedure tends to be embodied in written rules (as distinguished from unwritten traditions) to a greater extent than does English procedure, and partly because the legal profession in America is more numerous, more dispersed, and less specialized than in England. In any event, it seems a fair prediction that the results of the interchange of visits will be felt less quickly in America than in England.

Nevertheless, significant changes in the United States are reasonably to be anticipated. Optimism is justified by the fact that the restless American ferment for improvement in judicial administration is supported by a number of effective organizations and institutions. Law schools and their law reviews are among them, as are bar associations and their journals. Especially concerned with the appellate procedure are the annual Appellate Judges Seminar, the Conference of Chief Justices, and the Judicial Conference of the United States.

One development is already taking place, partly at least as a result of the stimulus provided by the project. It is the attempt of the United States Court of Appeals for the Second Circuit to increase the number of summary dispositions in simple, routine appeals, somewhat along the lines of English practice. This development is described in Chapter 4.

Sponsorship

Before the exchange of visits took place, the project as a whole was submitted to Lord Chancellor Kilmuir of England and Chief Justice Warren of the United States. Both of them warmly approved it and gave it all possible help.

On the English side, the study was sponsored by the British Council, which not only supplied some of the necessary funds, but also made many of the arrangements for the London visit. On the American side, where 50 quasi-sovereign states as well as the Federal Government were potentially involved, no official organization was at hand to play an equivalent role. The role was filled by the Institute of Judicial Administration, a private, nonprofit organization of judges, lawyers, and lay citizens devoted to improving the administration of justice (among its activities is sponsorship of the Appellate Judges Seminar mentioned above). Funds for the American share of the project were supplied to the Institute by the Walter E. Meyer Research Institute of Law, a private philanthropic foundation managed by trustees drawn mainly from the law schools of Columbia, Harvard, New York, and Yale Universities, which concentrates on improvements in the law.

Character of the Study

Two characteristics of the study are worthy of special note. First, it explored an area of comparative study which has received relatively little attention, considering its rather obvious importance. Instead of comparing practice in a common-law country with that of a civil-law country—the usual staple of comparative-law study—this project concentrated on a comparison within the common-law world. It did so with clear advantages: ease of communication, a common background of understanding, common goals and common traditions, and, most important of all, a substantial possibility of transferring useful ideas between nations.

The second noteworthy feature of the study was the fact that it was carried on mostly by judges and lawyers, rather than professors. There was an academic leavening in both groups, but most of the participants were practicing members of the profession. This was almost inevitable insofar as the English participation was concerned, for procedure, by and large, is not a subject of vital interest in the English universities. That is left mostly to judges and to practicing barristers and solicitors. The same situation prevails in the United States to a limited extent. While procedure is recognized as a respectable academic discipline in American law schools, judges and practicing lawyers tend to be looked upon as the real experts in that field. They know, as no professor can, the internal workings of the courts. Furthermore, effective communication with members of the English team seemed to demand that members of the American team should have roughly similar backgrounds and interests. Finally, in both nations, the prospect of achieving practical reforms—if any should be suggested by the study—seemed to depend largely upon the involvement of men who had the power and position to act.

The investigation of appellate procedure was originally envisaged as part of a larger comparative study of Anglo-American law. It still is. On both sides of the Atlantic, the present project appears to justify going ahead on other fronts—criminal trials, civil trials, judicial administration, and the like. This book, therefore, may turn out to be the first in a series.

Relation of Book to Project

In one sense, this book is the composite result of the thoughts and observations of all who participated in the project. In another sense it is an individual effort, the author bearing sole responsibility for all statements made and all opinions expressed.

Chapters 2 through 5 were prepared for the members of the English team in anticipation of their visit to the United States. They describe the four American courts visited by that team. While they do not purport to present a picture of every appellate court functioning in each of the 51 judicial systems of the United States (one for each state and one for the Federal Government), they do present, it is believed, a fair sampling of representative courts—enough, at least, to convey a feeling of how American appeals work in general.

Chapters 6 through 9 were prepared after the American visit to London. Describing the English courts, they are intended as a record of what was seen, heard, and learned by outside observers, operating at close range, under ideal conditions.

Both sets of chapters have been checked by persons intimately familiar with the courts described. Individual acknowledgments appear in connection with each description.

The final chapter, comparing appeals in the two nations, attempts to make explicit what is implicit in the earlier chapters. Because of its scope and nature, it could not be critically reviewed in detail by every person whose knowledge and experience are reflected in it. The most that was feasible was to receive suggestions from the heads of the two teams, Lord Evershed and Mr. Justice Brennan. Hence the author must stand accountable for any inaccuracies or misinterpretations the chapter may contain. On the other hand, whatever valuable insights it may contain are almost surely secondhand, being derived in very large part from comments by members of both teams and by many other persons who generously cooperated in the project.

CHAPTER TWO

A State Intermediate Appellate Court

THE APPELLATE DIVISION

OF THE NEW YORK SUPREME COURT

FIRST DEPARTMENT *

General Description and Place in Judicial Hierarchy

The Appellate Division of the New York Supreme Court, First Department, is an intermediate appellate court for both civil and criminal cases. It is one of four such courts in the state. The First Department covers geographically only two boroughs within the city of New York—Manhattan and the Bronx—but these, being heavily urban, commercial, and industrial, produce an immense amount of legal business, making this court an extremely busy one. The other three departments (centered respectively in Brooklyn, Albany, and Rochester), taking care of the remainder of the state, cover areas which are geographically much larger, but which, because of their partially rural character, produce far less legal business.[1]

Most cases reach the Appellate Division directly from the trial level. They come from the Supreme Court (important civil cases,

---

* Much of the information contained in this paper was furnished by the Honorable Bernard Botein, Presiding Justice, and Vincent A. Massi, Esq., clerk of the court. They have read this paper and furnished many valuable suggestions. The author wishes to here record his gratitude to them.

The following students of the School of Law of New York University assisted in preliminary "spadework" research on this and several other chapters of this book: Ara Asadourian, Phillip Glucksman, Andrew Hoge, Sherman Kendis, and Roger Soderberg. To them also the author wishes to express his thanks.

including law, equity, and divorce matters, and serious criminal cases); the Surrogate's Court (probate matters); and the Family Court (family matters other than separation, annulment, or divorce).[2]

Others reach the Appellate Division after they have already been through one stage of appellate review. These are the smaller civil cases (involving not more than $10,000 in controversy) originating in the Civil Court of the City of New York and appealed in the first instance to the Appellate Term of the Supreme Court. Further review in the Appellate Division is allowed only by permission of the Appellate Term or the Appellate Division, usually granted because of the presence of some significant question of law.[3]

Minor criminal cases, tried by the Criminal Court of the City of New York, also are appealed to the Appellate Term of the Supreme Court, but thereafter do not reach the Appellate Division. They go directly to the Court of Appeals if permission is granted by one of the judges of that court or by a justice of the Appellate Division.[4]

In civil cases, the Appellate Division hears appeals not only from final judgments, but also from interlocutory orders arising out of motions addressed to the pleadings, motions made in the course of discovery proceedings, and the like. These are appealable by the party aggrieved if they involve the merits of the action or affect substantial rights.[5] Determining whether a certain type of order meets this criterion is a matter of some difficulty, but once a decision is made, it becomes a precedent for other like orders. In other words, the appealability of such orders is not a matter of discretion exercised case by case, but a matter of right once the precedent has been established.[6]

In the more serious criminal cases tried in the Supreme Court, the defendant can appeal from a final judgment of conviction and from an order denying a motion to vacate a judgment of conviction.[7] The state also has a limited right of appeal—as from the sustaining of a demurrer to the indictment—but never where a verdict or judgment of not guilty has been rendered.[8]

The court sits only in Manhattan in a courthouse where all the judges have their chambers. In view of the limited geographical area covered, this creates no problem.

The court year runs from about the first week in September until the middle of June. It is divided into nine terms of three weeks each, separated by one week each month in which the court does not sit. That week is devoted exclusively to the writing of opinions, the holding of conferences, and other work in chambers.

Work is scheduled on three calendars:

The first, called the "General" or "Enumerated" Calendar, covers appeals from final judgments, civil or criminal, and interlocutory appeals presenting questions of substantive law. Arguments in these cases are heard from 2 P.M. to 6 P.M. on Wednesday, Thursday, and Friday afternoons during the first and third weeks of each term, and on Tuesday, Wednesday, Thursday, and Friday afternoons during the second week.

The second, described as the "Order" or "Nonenumerated Calendar" covers, in general, appeals from interlocutory orders presenting primarily questions of procedure—changes of venue, motions for more detailed pleadings, stays, orders for temporary alimony, and the like. This calendar is called on the first and third Tuesday of each term, beginning at 10 A.M. Most of these appeals are not argued orally, but are submitted on written briefs. The court discourages oral argument unless questions of substantive law are involved.

The third is the "Motion" Calendar, on which are placed miscellaneous applications, usually relating to pending appeals—requests to prosecute appeals in forma pauperis, applications for leave to appeal from the Appellate Term or to the Court of Appeals, and the like. This calendar is called by the Clerk of the Court (no Justices are present) immediately after the Order Calendar, beginning at 1 P.M. on the first and third Tuesday of each term. No oral arguments are permitted, these motions being decided solely upon the basis of the papers submitted.

Mondays are reserved for conferences, which start at 10 A.M.

and usually continue until late afternoon. In addition, special conferences are scheduled as needed.

Personnel

The court consists of eight [9] justices, but they do not sit en banc. Rather they sit in panels, five justices at a time. Assignments are made at the beginning of each term (but not announced publicly) in such a manner as to equalize the work of all members of the court. A justice may sit on Tuesday, be free the next day, sit on Thursday, and be free on Friday. On the average, he will sit eight days during each three-week term. By the end of the year, he will have heard approximately as many arguments as each of his colleagues and participated in the decision of an equal number of motions and unargued appeals. His "free" days, of course, are not really free, but are devoted to the examination of briefs and records, the preparation of opinions, and the study of opinions prepared by his colleagues.

The justices who compose the court are designated by the governor from among those who have been elected to the Supreme Court (14-year terms).[10] The one named as presiding justice serves in that capacity for the full term to which he was elected as Supreme Court justice, and receives a salary of $39,000 per year.[11] Those designated as associate justices serve for five-year terms, which are renewable, and receive salaries of $37,500 per year.[12]

The presiding justice carries about the same amount of appellate work as his colleagues and, in addition, the burdens of administration. These are not inconsiderable, because, along with the presiding justices of the three other Appellate Divisions of the state, he plays a very important role in the promulgation of Rules of Civil Practice and in the work of the state-wide Administrative Board of the Judicial Conference, thus in the administration of justice in the state generally.[13] With the advent of a reorganized court structure in the City of New York, his administrative burdens during the transition period will be very heavy indeed. One of his most important administrative duties within the court itself is to preside at the conferences of the justices—a job that requires great tact, patience, and equanimity. Under the new Administrative Act and the new Article 6 of the State Constitution, the entire court has heavy responsibilities for administering the lower courts of the First Department.

Each justice has the assistance of a law clerk and a stenographer. Unlike the law clerks found in most appellate courts, those serving in the Appellate Division are mature lawyers, 30 to 40 years of age usually, and receiving a salary of $13,500. They do not change from one year to another, but typically serve for several years.

Serving the entire court is a group of six "law assistants," who receive the same salaries as are paid to the law clerks and who generally resemble them in experience, age, and tenure. The functions they perform are described later, but it may be noted here that they make possible the focusing of eleven minds on the decision of each appeal presented to the court—that of the law assistant assigned to the case, those of the five justices responsible for the decision, and those of their five law clerks.

Volume and Scope of Work

During the court year ending June 30, 1960, the court decided 1,093 appeals on the General and Order Calendars, affirming in 610 cases, reversing in 211, and modifying in 111.[14] It decided 1,453 motions.[15] Finally, it disposed of many miscellaneous matters, including disciplinary proceedings, submitted controversies, and the like.

During this period, the court produced 75 per curiam opinions and 119 regular opinions, as well as a great number of memorandum decisions and affirmances without opinion.[16]

In terms of the number of full opinions written, the Appellate Division, First Department, is not an unusually heavy producer. It is exceeded, for example, by the United States Court of Appeals for the Second Circuit and the New York Court of Appeals. In terms of the number of appeals decided, however, it is busier than any other appellate division in the state, and probably busier than any other appellate court in the nation.

Since each justice participates in five-eighths of the entire caseload of the court, he is involved in the decision of about 700 appeals per year or almost 80 per month. In addition his share of motions is about 900 per year or 100 per month.

As for the scope of review, the court considers questions of fact as well as questions of law. It will not, however, substitute its judgment for the verdict of a jury or the finding of an administrative agency, but will limit itself to inquiring whether there is substantial evidence to support it. When reviewing cases tried by a judge alone, it will accord respect to his superior opportunity to determine the credibility of witnesses and will ordinarily limit itself to reviewing the inferences and value judgments made by him.

The court follows the usual American pattern in interpreting statutes (using legislative history, when available), in overruling its own precedents when they are deemed to have outlived their usefulness, and in granting new trials in criminal as well as civil cases.

Documents on Appeal

Each side is required to serve on the other side and file a brief (or written argument) with the court. That of the appellant is designed to indicate the nature of the case, the proceedings below, the issues presented on appeal, the reasons why the judgment should be reversed or modified, and the authorities (statutory and case-made) justifying that result.[17] It must be served and filed within 20 days after the record on appeal is filed.[18] The brief of the respondent is defensive, arguing that the judgment below should be affirmed and giving reasons and authorities in support of that position. It must be served and filed within 15 days of the service of appellant's brief.[19] Sometimes the appellant files a reply brief, due five days later,[20] disputing the points made in the respondent's brief. Counsel are not limited as to the length of their briefs.

Underlying and supporting the briefs is a record on appeal, prepared, served, and filed by the appellant.[21] Its purpose is to reproduce the formal papers used in the court below—pleadings, judgment, etc.—and so much of the evidence as is relevant to the questions raised on appeal. Almost invariably, however, this limitation is disregarded by counsel and not enforced by the court, with the result that many needlessly long records are submitted.

Both briefs and records on appeal are ordinarily required to be printed.[22] The cost is upward of $3 or $4 per page. Provision is made, in appropriate circumstances, for some appeals to be taken in forma pauperis or on typewritten records.[23] Nevertheless, the sheer mechanical costs are so high as to discourage many appeals.[24]

Nineteen copies of each document are required to be filed,[25] allowing one for each justice who will participate, one for each law clerk of each participating justice, and one for the law assistant working on the case, as well as a number of spare copies which will ultimately be distributed to law libraries.

The prescribed time schedule for the preargument stages of an appeal from the entry of judgment below is as follows: [26]

30 days	notice of appeal filed
20 days	record on appeal filed
20 days	appellant's brief filed
15 days	respondent's brief filed
5 days	reply brief filed
28 days	either party may notice a case for the first Tuesday of a term on 28 days' notice

TOTAL   118 days

Note: if oral argument is desired, the clerk must be notified 12 days before the term for which the appeal has been noticed.

If the appellant desires speedier disposition, he can shorten the timetable considerably by taking less time than is allowed him.

Despite the foregoing schedule, opposing counsel are likely to be indulgent toward each other in the matter of meeting deadlines, and often the court will extend time on a showing of good cause. Once all briefs are in, however, a case is reached for argument promptly—within one to three weeks. After argument, the decision is reached with equal dispatch—within two and one-half to three weeks, usually. When the court recesses at the end of June each year, it ordinarily has disposed of all of its cases. Almost never is any case carried under consideration during the summer recess.

The six law assistants mentioned earlier play an important role in getting cases ready for decision. Before the beginning of each term, the chief law assistant assigns to each of the other five law assistants approximately one-fifth of the cases to be considered that term. This usually amounts to some 22 appeals per month or about 200 per year. Motions are also assigned to law assistants except those involving permission for leave to appeal to or from the Appellate Division, rehearings, and attorney disciplinary matters. All of these are handled by the justices directly.

With respect to each case assigned to him, the law assistant prepares a memorandum outlining the issues, the contentions of the parties, the relevant authorities, and his recommendation as to disposition. In order to do this, he studies the briefs of both sides and the record to the extent necessary. In view of the fact that the briefs in a typical appeal are likely to run 50 to 60 pages in length and the record on appeal another 350 or 400 pages, the job of merely studying the papers submitted is a very large one. In addition, the law assistant may and frequently does conduct independent research into the legal authorities when he is not satisfied with the presentations made in the briefs by counsel. He embodies his conclusions in a document which ordinarily runs from two to six typewritten, double-spaced pages in length. If the case is complicated, the memorandum may be considerably longer.

This memorandum is then sent to the chief law assistant, who examines it for substance and form and suggests such changes as he considers desirable. If he and the draftsman of the memorandum are in accord, copies of the finished product are sent to the five justices who will be participating in the decision of the appeal. If there is disagreement, the chief law assistant prepares his own supplemental memorandum and both it and the original memorandum are circulated to the justices. All memoranda are confidential, neither published nor open to public inspection.

Prior to hearing oral argument, the justices may supplement their preliminary study of the briefs submitted by counsel by examining these memoranda prepared by the law assistants. Some of the justices, however, pay little attention to the memoranda at this point, preferring to rely upon their own study and research and upon the assistance of their own law clerks.

Oral Argument

Motions are never argued orally. Appeals may or may not be. About half of those on the Order Calendar (practice matters called on the first and third Tuesdays of each term) are argued orally, whereas about 80 percent of those on the General Calendar are argued orally. If both sides are willing, they may "submit"—that is to say, agree to dispense with oral argument and have the case decided upon the papers alone. This may be done at any time after the appeal is docketed, without waiting for it to be reached in regular order.[27]

It may also be done inadvertently by the failure of counsel to request oral argument. Prior to the time that a case is reached for hearing, the attorneys for both sides must indicate whether they wish to submit or have oral argument. If they desire oral argument, they state how much time will be required. In enumerated appeals, each side is allowed 60 minutes,[28] but the expectation is that neither will ask for more than 15 to 30 minutes. (In nonenumerated appeals, each side is allowed only 15 minutes.) On the basis of the statements of counsel, the clerk makes up the list of cases for each day. He attempts to schedule enough cases to keep the court occupied for the full four hours that it will be sitting, but no more than will actually be reached. Ordinarily, therefore, he schedules seven or eight cases a day. Two or three of these very likely will be submitted on the call of the calendar for the day. Sometimes, in order to dispose of all cases noticed for a given term, one or two additional days of argument are scheduled. When a particular case is called, the lawyer for the appellant must be present and ready to proceed. If he is not, his appeal will be marked "submitted," regardless of previous indications of a desire to argue it, and, since in such circumstances the attorney for the respondent ordinarily will not insist upon being heard, the court will move on to the next case.

If the lawyer for the appellant is present and ready, he will be held to the time previously indicated by him to the clerk as necessary. He may, however, state at the outset that he will reserve part of the time for a reply to his opponent.

In view of the fact that the justices have already read the briefs, the attorney for the appellant does not have to spend as much time as he would otherwise in describing the case and the questions raised on appeal. All he needs to do is refresh the court's recollection as to those matters, and he can devote his major effort to an attempt to persuade the court that the judgment below should be reversed or modified. On the other hand, a good deal of his time is likely to be devoted to answering questions put by the justices and pursuing lines of thought indicated by them as being of special interest. However much of his time is thus absorbed, he must conclude his presentation in the time allotted. The court may, as a matter of grace, extend that time, but counsel cannot count on it. Ordinarily, counsel is not permitted to read to the court extensive excerpts from the record on appeal or from legal authorities.

The argument of counsel for the respondent follows the same pattern: he, too, must refrain from reading to the court; he must finish within the time allotted; and he may be subjected to extensive questioning by the court. The same conditions also prevail with respect to the reply argument, if any, by counsel for the appellant.

When the arguments are concluded, decision is reserved. No attempt is made (save in the most unusual circumstances, as where an election is being contested and the matter cannot wait) to reach an immediate decision. If any discussions take place at or shortly after the conclusion of oral arguments, they are informal and tentative, amounting to no more than an exchange of preliminary reactions between the justices involved.

Assignment of Cases

Each appeal becomes the special responsibility of one of the justices for the purpose of initially reporting on it to his colleagues. This is accomplished by a rotational system, which may be described as follows:

The five chairs behind the bench in the courtroom are occupied by the justices in order of seniority. The center one is occupied by the justice presiding—not necessarily the presiding justice, but the senior justice present; the chair to his right, by the next senior justice; the chair to his left, by the third senior justice; the chair to the far right, by the justice fourth in order of seniority; and the chair to the far left, by the junior justice. Looking at the bench from the front (facing the justices) the chairs are numbered "1" through "5" from right to left.

Cases are assigned to the chairs in numerical sequence. If on the last previous day of argument, the last submitted (not argued) case fell to chair number "3," the first case argued (not submitted) on the next day of hearings will go to chair number "4," the next to chair number "5," the next to chair number "1," and so on. When all of the argued cases have been assigned in this manner, the submitted cases are assigned in like fashion, the first of the day going to the chair next in order after the chair that received the last argued case. If that case fell to chair number "1," the first submitted case falls to chair number "2," the next to chair number "3," and so forth. Thus, over the course of a year, each justice receives approximately the same number of assignments of cases as his colleagues.

No justice knows for any appreciable time in advance of oral argument which cases will become "his." That does not become apparent until the calendar is called at the beginning of each session. Despite the fact that most of the cases placed on the calendar are those in which oral argument has been requested, some of these are "submitted" nevertheless on the briefs alone at this time. The lawyers may have had second thoughts about the necessity or desirability of an oral presentation, or they may be engaged in appearances before other courts, or they may have other reasons for relying on their briefs alone. Whatever the cause, not all of the cases scheduled for oral argument are actually heard. Thus it is only after the calendar call has been completed that the justices know which of the argued cases will become their special responsibility.

As for submitted appeals, the justices do not become aware of their special assignments until the end of each day of argument. At that time, these appeals are assigned to the chairs on the rotational basis just described.

Motions are also divided between the justices, but on a somewhat different basis. Those seeking rehearings or leave to appeal to the Court of Appeals go to the justices who originally reported on the cases involved, regardless of whether they are sitting on the day when these motions are submitted. They then report only to the other justices who heard the cases originally. All other motions are divided equally between the justices sitting on the day when they are submitted.

The Preliminary Stage of Decision-making

After an appeal has been argued or submitted, the crucial work of reaching a decision lies ahead.

In the first instance, primary responsibility falls on the justice to whom the particular case has been assigned, for he is required to report on the case to his colleagues. Since his report is expected at a conference scheduled for the Monday following argument or submission, he has to get to work immediately. Part of his "free" time is already preempted by the necessity of attending conferences, hearing arguments, and reading briefs in advance for cases about to be argued.

The extent to which a justice must study the briefs and records on appeal in cases assigned to him for reporting depends on how much study he has previously given them. In cases which have been argued, he has already done part of his "homework," seeking to learn at least enough about the case to be able to appreciate the issues involved and to follow the arguments of counsel. In other words, he has been twice exposed to the case before— once during the preliminary study of briefs, and again during oral argument—but the extent of the exposure may have been either heavy or light.

At some point, the justice must make an intensive study of the briefs of both sides. That is an inescapable part of his responsibility, for he must thoroughly understand the issues raised and the grounds relied on for reversal or modification of the decision below. Even if the case has been orally argued, the task is unavoidable, for it is the general understanding of the legal profession that appeals will not be decided upon oral argument alone, that briefs will be conscientiously studied by the court.

As for the record on appeal, that presents a different problem. It may or may not have to be examined. Certainly under the adversary system, in which the presumption is indulged that each side is represented by competent counsel, there is no responsibility on the court to independently search the record to see whether any errors were committed below which would warrant reversal or modification of the decision. The justices have too much work to allow them to embark on such an operation; and if they did, their efforts would be resented by counsel. When it is remembered that many records contain masses of irrelevant material, unrelated to any issue raised on appeal (for example, evidence on the question of damages in an auto accident case when the appeal relates solely to liability), the futility of any attempt at a complete review by the court of every record on appeal becomes obvious. Indeed, it would be physically impossible for the justices of the Appellate Division to read in their entirety all of the records on appeal in all cases in which they participate.[29]

After the reporting justice has studied the briefs and record to the extent he deems necessary, he must resolve in his own mind the questions left open. This usually involves a reading of at least some of the cases, statutes, and authorities which have been cited by counsel. While the court may be content with statements of counsel as to what the record shows (if counsel are agreed), it can hardly be content to rely exclusively upon counsel for what the governing law is. That is the court's peculiar province and responsibility—to clarify, elucidate, and sometimes mold the law. Frequently there is a dispute between counsel as to the rule or rules that ought to govern, which can be resolved only by a judicial examination of the authorities. Sometimes, moreover, a point has not been adequately briefed by counsel. If so, the court will either have to pronounce the law (or at least decide the case) on the basis of research which is recognized to be inadequate, or it will have to do the job of research itself. Initially (but only initially) that job falls upon the reporting justice, since he must make up his own mind before he can recommend to his colleagues the disposition which the court as a whole should make. In this labor, as in all of his other labors in chambers or in the library, he has the assistance of his law clerk, to be used as he sees fit.

In short, a justice, in preparing to report, has to go through virtually the same intellectual labors as would be involved if he were writing the opinion of the court. Not only must he study the papers submitted and conduct or supervise such independent research as he deems necessary, he must also consider the equities and make whatever policy and value judgments are called for. Until he has done so, he is not prepared to recommend to his colleagues, even tentatively, the disposition which should be made by the court. The only thing he does not have to do is to write an opinion. His job at this stage is complete with the preparation of notes which will be used by him as the basis for an oral presentation at the Monday conference. He already has in his possession, for such use as he wishes to make of it, the memorandum on the case prepared by one of the law assistants.

Such is the job of a justice with respect to the cases assigned to him. Since each term that he sits he will have assigned to him about 15 appeals from the General Calendar and an additional four or five cases from the Order Calendar as well as about 20 motions from the Motion Calendar, it can be readily seen that he has many reports to prepare in the short time available to him. If a particular case presents special difficulties, he can postpone reporting until a later conference, but if the appeals and motions are "routine," he is expected to be ready with reports on them by the Monday following the date of their submission or argument.

Heavy as the work just described must be, it is not the full measure of the justice's responsibility. He must also be prepared to vote on the appeals and motions which have been assigned to the other justices. Since each of them has been assigned the same number of cases as himself, he has the job of reviewing each term some 60 or 65 appeals as well as 80-odd motions. This seems a Herculean task, involving, as it does, the consideration of an average of about two appeals and three motions per day, Saturdays and Sundays included. All this is superimposed upon the justice's obligation to give reports on the cases assigned to him, to participate in long conferences (several hours most Mondays), to spend some 32 hours on the bench listening to arguments, and to spend additional time in preparation therefor!

Although obviously no justice is able to give to the cases assigned to his colleagues quite the same amount of attention he gives to cases which are his own, his responsibility with respect to those cases is not very much lighter. He must study each one to the point where he feels confident of the result that should be reached. That will be his basis for voting upon it in conference.

The Conference of Judges

The Monday conference is held in a special conference room with the justices seated at a round table.

It is divided into two parts. The first is devoted to a consideration of those matters heard or submitted during the previous week. The judges in attendance shift as each day's cases come up for discussion. Those who were sitting on Tuesday participate in the discussion of cases argued or submitted on that day; those sitting on Wednesday participate in the discussion of cases argued or submitted on that day, and so on.

The second part of the conference is devoted to matters held over from previous weeks, administrative problems, and, most important, opinions which have been written in cases considered earlier. All of the justices who compose the court participate in this part of the conference, with the presiding justice presiding.

In the first part of the conference, as each appeal or motion is called for discussion, the justice to whom it was assigned makes his report, recommending the action which he thinks the court should take, with his reasons.

He speaks with no special authority about that appeal; no other justice yields to his judgment because the appeal was assigned to him; and no undue respect is paid to his views or recommendation. In a word he has no "lien" intellectual or otherwise on the appeal assigned to him. He is but one of five justices, each of them exercising independent judgment, and equally responsible for the decision of the appeal.[30]

Thereafter the case is open for general discussion. After the justices have carried on the discussion as long as they desire (a few seconds or a few minutes or an hour), it may be apparent that further consideration is necessary. If so, the matter is postponed to a future conference. If not, it is put to a vote. If the vote unanimously sustains the position of the reporting justice, and if it affirms the decision below, that is the end of the case. Ordinarily no opinion will be written; the result merely will be published in what is known within the courthouse as an "ANOPAC" ("Affirmed; no opinion; all concur").

If there is a dissent or if the vote is to reverse the decision below, there will be an opinion, but it may take any one of three forms: a full opinion, a per curiam opinion, or a memorandum. Ordinarily the justice who presented the report writes the opinion of the court if he is in the majority and any opinion is to be written. If he is in the minority, he ordinarily will write whatever dissenting opinion is to be written. In that case, the majority opinion will have to be written by someone else, usually a volunteer or the junior justice in the majority.

After the current cases have been disposed of in the manner indicated, all justices of the court take places around the table and the second part of the conference begins. At this time, matters postponed or adjourned from previous conferences are considered. The procedure is the same as that described above.

Then comes the consideration of opinions prepared in cases considered and voted upon earlier. These have been distributed in advance by their authors to all of the other justices. Again full discussion may ensue, and criticisms and suggestions may be freely offered. Sometimes at this point, a previously dissenting view may be converted by discussion into the prevailing view, and an opinion prepared as a flaming dissent may become the opinion of the court. Or (which is more likely) it may be toned down to represent a consensus or even shrunken to a memorandum merely expressing a result acceptable to a majority of the justices. No justice is irrevocably committed to a position until a final vote has been taken and the decision publicly announced. The only justices who vote on an opinion are those who participated in the hearing of the case (although questions of general policy are discussed among all of the justices).

Whatever the course of the discussion and whatever its result in a particular case, the impact of the conference upon the decision-making process is profound. In the words of a former justice previously quoted:

> None of us labors under the delusion that he knows everything. Each makes his own contribution. Each has a hospitable receptivity to the viewpoints of the others. Perhaps the spirit which, in the main, pervades the consultation room is best exemplified by the verse from Isaiah: "Come now and let us reason together."

It is difficult to convey an adequate picture of the stimulating impact of mind upon mind, of how, as the discussion proceeds, as searching questions are put and answered, the process of synthesizing the views of the justices makes itself manifest, errors are squeezed out, the mists of misapprehensions and misunderstandings are cleared away, and common ground so often reached.

Those are the most exhilarating experiences in appellate court work. On the whole, I believe it may fairly be stated that the attitude of the justices of our court is akin to the view expressed by Benjamin Franklin at the Constitutional Convention of 1787, when he said: "We are sent here to consult, not to contend with each other; and declarations of a fixed opinion and of determined resolution, never to change it, neither enlighten nor convince us. For, having lived long, I have experienced many instances of being obliged, by better information or fuller consideration, to change opinions, even on important subjects which I once thought right but found to be otherwise. It is, therefore, that the older I grow the more apt I am to doubt my own judgment and to pay more respect to the judgment of others." (Carl Van Doren, *The Great Rehearsal* [1948], 76, 168).[31]

As already indicated, opinions are not written on all appeals. Some cases are disposed of merely by published announcements of the result. While the Appellate Division of the First Department follows this practice less frequently than its sister courts in other departments, it nevertheless leaves some of its decisions unexplained. Such a decision does not indicate concurrence with the reasoning of the court below, but only with the result reached there. If the Appellate Division wishes to indicate its line of reasoning without writing an opinion, it may say that the judgment is affirmed "on the opinion below," or words to that effect.

If an opinion is rendered, it is likely to take the form of a memorandum opinion. This, as its name implies, is a very brief statement (usually not more than about 100 words) of the reasons for the court's holding. It may or may not cite authorities and it may or may not be accompanied by an equally brief dissenting memorandum (in which case the votes of the justices are recorded). In the year ending June 30, 1960, 806 such opinions were rendered.[32]

If fuller treatment is desired, an opinion can take either of two forms: regular or per curiam. The difference between them is not easy to define, but this much can be said: a per curiam is anonymous, whereas a regular opinion bears the name of its author; and a per curiam is ordinarily shorter than a regular opinion (but longer than a memorandum opinion). In the year ending June 30, 1960, 119 regular opinions and 75 per curiams were rendered. In addition 51 dissenting and four concurring opinions were rendered.[33]

The writing of an opinion involves much the same type of work as goes into the study of a case for purposes of reporting. If it is to take the form of a memorandum, very little may need to be done. Indeed, the memorandum may have already been dictated during the conference. If, however, it is to take the form of a per curiam or a regular opinion, more work ordinarily is required. Further research may be necessary, as well as more careful draftsmanship. Language now becomes important, for the opinion will become a precedent guiding future decisions not only in the courts below but also in the Appellate Division, First Department, itself. Whatever work is involved, the justice has available the services of his law clerk to help him.

After the job has been completed, the resulting opinion is considered in conference in the manner already described. When approved, that fact is made known in the daily *New York Law Journal* and copies of the opinion (or opinions) are made available to counsel by the clerk of the court. This usually takes place within about eighteen days from the time of oral argument or submission. It is unusual for more than three weeks to elapse. The total time between the filing of a notice of appeal and the decision ranges from about five to ten months.

PUBLICATION OF OPINIONS

All decisions of the court are published, whether in the form of regular, per curiam, or memorandum opinions or mere announcements of results in particular cases. They appear not only in the official *New York Reports* (with advance sheets) but also in the unofficial *New York Supplement* (also with advance sheets).

Finality of Decisions

Rehearings, though possible,[34] are rarely permitted. If the court, in its discretion, grants a rehearing, it reconsiders the case on the papers alone without oral reargument.

Further review is possible in the New York Court of Appeals under the conditions indicated in the description of that court.

CHAPTER THREE

A State Court of Last Resort

THE NEW YORK COURT OF APPEALS *

General Description and Place in Judicial Hierarchy

The Court of Appeals is the highest court of New York for both civil and criminal cases.[1] Its jurisdiction is purely appellate, and none of its judges do any trial work.[2]

Most cases reach the court from one of the four Appellate Divisions of the Supreme Court (intermediate appellate courts). This means that they have already been through at least one appeal, so that the proceeding in the Court of Appeals amounts to a second, sometimes even a third, review. The following cases are reviewable as a matter of right: [3]

(1) those in which the Appellate Division reversed or modified the decision below;
(2) those in which there was a dissent in the Appellate Division; and
(3) those in which the construction of a statute of the state or the United States Constitution was directly involved.

Other cases go up only by permission of the Appellate Division concerned or the Court of Appeals itself.[4]

A few cases reach the Court of Appeals from courts other than the Appellate Divisions. Some come from the Appellate Term of the Supreme Court, First Department, which acts as an appellate court for minor criminal cases tried by the Criminal Court of the City of New York. Further review is possible in the Court of Ap-

---

* This paper is based in part upon information furnished by the Hon. Charles S. Desmond, Chief Judge of New York, to whom the author wishes to express his gratitude.

peals if permission is granted by one of its judges. Some come directly and as of right from trial courts—for example, where the death penalty was imposed in a homicide case [5]—or where the only question involved is the constitutional validity of a state or federal statute.[6]

Appeals as of Right and Applications for Leave to Appeal

Some appeals taken as of right to the court involve questions of obvious importance. Others are of such nature that it is hard to justify their consideration by the highest court of the state. If the court had discretion to screen appeals now taken as of right, it is probable that it would reject a substantial number of them.[7]

A motion for leave to appeal in a civil case is submitted in written form, accompanied by a supporting brief. The other party has the privilege of submitting a brief in opposition and usually avails himself of it.[8] Oral argument is not permitted.[9]

While all judges receive copies of all papers submitted, a particular judge is assigned primary responsibility for dealing with each application. Assignments are usually made in rotation, with Judge A receiving application number one, Judge B application number two, and so on. The assigned judge studies the papers and prepares a report—six or seven pages in length usually—recommending that the motion be granted or denied.[10] Copies are circulated to the other judges, and when they meet in conference (a procedure to be described later), a vote is taken. If at least two judges feel that permission to appeal should be granted, the other judges usually, though not always, accede to their wishes and the motion is granted unanimously.[11]

At one time it was the philosophy of the court that leave to appeal should be granted only in cases of general public importance. The court seemed to consider that its primary function was to clarify, elucidate, and develop the law, and that it did not have time or resources sufficient to see that justice was done in every case.[12] The view today seems to be somewhat different. Leave to appeal will be granted, of course, when a question of general importance is presented, but it will also be granted if there is some probability that the decision below should be reversed, whether or not the question involved is one of general importance.[13] In this respect the criteria used by the court are in sharp contrast to those used by the United States Supreme Court in passing upon roughly equivalent petitions for certiorari.

During the last court year, the Court of Appeals decided about 500 motions for leave to appeal in civil cases. One hundred and twenty-four were granted, the rest denied.

Applications for leave to appeal in criminal cases, other than capital cases, are made to individual judges. In the year 1960–61, 112 criminal appeals were heard. Seven were capital cases, which came to the court as of right; 24 came by permission of a justice of the Appellate Division; and the remaining 81 came by permission of a judge of the Court of Appeals.

In addition to deciding appeals as of right and appeals by permission, the court decides about 200 miscellaneous motions a year. These relate to pending appeals—applications for extensions of time to serve briefs, for permission to dispense with printing, and the like.

Time and Place of Holding Court

The court sits only in Albany. It is empowered to sit elsewhere in the state, but does not do so despite the fact that a great many of its cases come from New York City and Buffalo (150 and 300 miles respectively from Albany).

The court year runs from September through June, with arguments being heard 18 weeks during that period. Occasionally special sessions are held in addition. In accordance with a schedule prepared in the fall, the court sits to hear appeals for two or three weeks; then recesses for three or four weeks; and then reconvenes to hear more appeals; then recesses again, and so forth. When hearing appeals, the judges occupy chambers in the courthouse in Albany. During recess periods, they return to their respective homes throughout the state, where each has a set of chambers in which he does most of his "homework" and writes most of his opinions.

The court always sits en banc, all seven members participating. During a week when it is in session, arguments are heard every day, Monday through Thursday, starting at 2:00 P.M. and ending at about 7:00 P.M. Usually six or seven cases are heard each day.

Personnel

The chief judge and the six associate judges are elected officials who run for office on party tickets and serve 14-year terms, subject, however, to mandatory retirement at age 70.[14] Very often a man goes on the court initially by appointment of the governor to fill a vacancy when another judge dies, retires, or resigns. In that event, the appointee must stand for election at the next general election, when he may (or may not) be opposed by a candidate from another political party. After he has served a full term, however, in all probability he will receive the endorsement of both parties and so be reelected without opposition. Sometimes the men appointed or elected to the court have had prior judicial experience, sometimes not.

The judges are the best paid of all American appellate judges.[15] The chief judge receives an annual salary of $39,000 plus an allowance of $5,000 in lieu of expenses. The associate judges receive salaries of $35,500 plus $5,000 in allowances.[16]

Each judge, including the chief judge, has one or two law clerks. Most, but not all, are recent law school graduates. They are appointed by the judges individually, and ordinarily do not serve for longer than a year or two. The average salary is about $7,000.

The chief judge is the administrative head of the court. He presides not only at the hearing of arguments, but also at the conferences of the judges. Unlike the presiding judges of some courts, however, he does not have the power to assign the writing of opinions or memoranda on the cases heard. That, as will become clear later, is by tradition handled on a rotational basis.

In addition to supervising the internal operations of the court, the chief judge has extremely important functions to perform as chairman of the administrative board and of the judicial conference of the state. As such, he is "Chief Judge of the State of New

York" and "the chief judicial officer of the unified court system," [17] with authority and responsibility for supervision of the entire judicial system of the state.[18]

Scope and Nature of Review

In capital cases, the court reviews both law and fact.[19] In other cases, it is restricted to questions of law.[20] The distinction, however, is a subtle one. There is no doubt that the Court of Appeals, like other American appellate courts, must in a sense deal with questions of fact when it is passing upon the sufficiency of evidence to sustain a judgment, civil or criminal.[21]

The court follows the standard American approach in deciding appeals: it uses legislative history, where available,[22] in interpreting statutes; it grants new trials in criminal as well as civil cases; and it overrules its own previous decisions when it believes that they have outlived their usefulness.

It has been more vigorous than most American appellate courts in upsetting precedents. Many of its cases overrule prior decisions, some of them involving common-law doctrines of ancient lineage. Its action in this regard must be appraised in light of the fact that, unlike the Supreme Court of the United States, the Court of Appeals ordinarily deals with rules which are susceptible of legislative correction, not constitutional doctrines which can be corrected only by constitutional amendment or judicial revision.

Documents on Appeal

Preliminary documents submitted to the court on applications for leave to appeal have already been described.

The additional, and more important, documents which deal with the merits follow much the same pattern as those submitted to the Appellate Divisions. Again briefs are filed by both sides, along with a record on appeal. If, as is usually the case, one appeal has already been heard below, the decision rendered upon it is included with the papers setting forth the proceedings in the trial courts. There may or may not be a reasoned opinion from below, containing a judicial definition of the issues, their solution, and the authorities relied upon. It is not the American custom for trial judges to render such opinions; they operate instead through instructions to juries, or, in nonjury cases, findings of fact and conclusions of law. These are included in the record on appeal, but they do not always serve the same function for an appellate court as reasoned opinions would serve. Furthermore, even if the case has been once heard upon appeal, there still may be no reasoned opinion. The vast majority of cases decided by the appellate divisions result in nothing more than memorandum or per curiam opinions.

Briefs and the record on appeal ordinarily are required to be printed, although the court can and frequently does grant permission to proceed on the basis of typewritten or mimeographed copies.[23] New York is one of a minority of states that adhere to printing as a normal requirement. A great many state appellate courts and some United States Courts of Appeals have enormously reduced the mechanical costs of appellate review by dispensing with printing in favor of substitute, cheaper methods of reproduction.[24]

Eighteen copies of each brief and record on appeal are required to be filed, except when the court orders otherwise. This allows one for each judge as well as a number of extra copies for distribution to law school and bar association libraries.[25]

Oral Argument

A case is reached for oral argument one to three months after the appeal is taken. It takes about this long, on the average, for the record on appeal and the briefs to be served and filed.

At the time that arguments on any given day begin, each judge knows which case or cases are assigned to him. This has been determined by lot the night before. Each case to be heard is numbered, and the numbers are placed in a hat, from which the clerk of the court draws them. The first case of the court year goes to the chief judge, the second to the senior associate judge and so on. The drawing continues evening after evening during sittings, so that each appeal becomes the special charge of one of the members of the court.[26]

The judge to whom a given case has been assigned knows—and his colleagues also know, though counsel do not—that he will write a special report on it for his fellow judges, and that, if his views prevail, he will also write the majority opinion (if any) for the court. Because of his special responsibility, he may require his law clerks to be present during the argument so that they will be in a better position to assist him when the time for research and writing comes.

In the other cases to be heard at the same time, however, he will probably count on getting his first impressions from the oral arguments (except as he may recall some cases from having previously considered applications for leave to appeal). He will have before him a one-page memorandum on each case, prepared by a law clerk, outlining very briefly the nature of the case, the issues involved, and the jurisdictional problems, if any, presented.[27] He will also have before him the briefs in each case, but he probably will not have read them in advance. Their chief utility at this point is for marginal note-taking during the course of argument.

In criminal cases, each side may be allowed 30 minutes; in civil cases, one hour. Rarely, however, is that much time used, for the court ordinarily hears six or seven cases in a period of four or five hours. The average time is about 25 minutes for each side. This is true in spite of the fact that in some cases there is questioning from the court. The judges resent any attempt by counsel to read in extenso from the record, the briefs, or the authorities relied on. What they want is a brief explanation of what the case is about, what the issues are, and how counsel thinks they should be resolved.[28]

Some appeals are not argued orally at all, but submitted on the briefs. This happens in about five percent of the cases heard on the merits.

The Judges' Reports

Ordinarily no attempt is made by the judges during or immediately after oral argument to reach decisions. Any conversations they have then are likely to be entirely casual and informal.

Each judge works individually on the cases assigned to him, with the goal of preparing reports for his colleagues which will recommend affirmance, reversal, or modification. With the assistance of his law clerks, he studies the briefs, and, to the extent necessary, the records on appeal; he conducts such independent research as he deems desirable. He may also discuss cases with his fellow judges, although this is not likely to happen except when the judges are together in Albany during argument weeks. During weeks of recess, when they are working in their home chambers, communications have to be carried on by mail or telephone.

When satisfied as to the result that ought to be reached in a particular case, the assigned judge writes a report, giving his recommendations and his reasons. This may turn out to be the first draft of the opinion of the court. Copies are circulated by mail or messenger to the other judges.

Any one of them at this point may prepare a separate report on the same case, arguing for a different conclusion. If so, it is circulated in the same manner as the original report.

All reports are confidential and not open to public inspection.

Meanwhile, all of the judges devote to cases which are not assigned to them such study as they consider necessary to inform the votes they will cast during conference.

Conference

Every morning except Friday when the court is in session in Albany, the judges meet in conference in the library of the courthouse from about 9:30 A.M. to 1:00 P.M. Law clerks as well as members of the public are excluded.[29]

The main purpose of these conferences is to discuss cases in which reports have been submitted. The reporting judge leads off the discussion by orally summarizing his report; then, if any other reports have been submitted on the case, their authors summarize them.[30] Thereafter the case is open for general discussion, with judges freely indicating their views, whether they have submitted written reports or not. After they have devoted as much discussion as they wish to the case (this may be virtually none or a great deal), a vote is taken. If all or a majority support the views expressed by the reporting judge, he thereby acquires the responsibility of preparing the opinion for the court.[31] If, on the other hand, the majority is against the reporting judge, he will write, if anything, only a dissenting or concurring opinion. One of the judges in the majority will write the court's opinion. If its view is based upon a report which was circulated in advance, the judge who wrote it will write the court's opinion, but if the majority view is predicated solely on oral discussion, the judge who first enunciated the prevailing view will write the opinion.[32] Since discussion generally follows the order of seniority, this very likely will be the senior judge representing the prevailing view.

In addition to considering reports on pending cases, the conference also takes up motions of all kinds, including applications for leave to appeal and motions for rehearing. Since, with respect to these matters, there is also a reporting judge (the same rotational system prevails), discussion tends to follow the same pattern as on reports. Because of the subject matter involved, however, less time is necessary.

Opinions in cases previously considered ordinarily require little discussion in conference. The opinions having been circulated and considered in advance, all that normally needs to be done is to record the final votes of the judges.

An unusual feature of the conferences is that they are tape-recorded and transcribed, so that each judge, when preparing opinions assigned to him, has in readily available form the orally expressed views of his colleagues. Furthermore, when a case has to be considered at a second or third conference, the earlier discussion is available for ready reference.

Opinions

After a case has been voted on in conference, the opinion of the court remains to be drafted. The judge charged with the task may be able to use a report previously written without substantial change. On the other hand, there may be no written report representing the majority view, or if there is one, the judge drafting the opinion may feel impelled to make substantial corrections, revisions, additions, deletions, and elaborations, or even to start afresh. No accurate generalizations are possible here. Much depends upon how elaborately the original report or reports were prepared, and upon the viewpoints expressed during conference.

Not infrequently the judge drafting the opinion will attempt to take account of differing points of view. This may involve informal discussions with some of his colleagues and the interchange of memoranda. It may also involve redrafting. The opinion ultimately produced may be a composite, not precisely representing the views of the judge whose name it bears.[33] Indeed, it may be so far from representing those views or the views of any other member of the court that it will be labeled a per curiam opinion, its authorship remaining anonymous.[34]

It is also possible that the judge in charge of a case will decide that it does not merit a full opinion. In that case, he will prepare a brief per curiam or memorandum, again not carrying his name. If this occurs, the final decision will not reflect the extensive labor that may have gone into it.

Once the majority opinion, whatever its form, is in such shape that it satisfies its author, he distributes copies to all colleagues. They are privileged, of course, to disagree; and any judge who feels so inclined may draft and circulate a separate opinion, dissenting or concurring as the case may be. Such an opinion may prove so persuasive that other judges change their votes. If enough of them do, the document which started out as a dissent or concurrence may be converted into the opinion of the court.

After all opinions have been distributed and considered, the case comes up again at an Albany conference, where the final vote is recorded. Thereafter, nothing remains to be done but file the opinions with the clerk, thus formally promulgating the decision. The opinions are not read or summarized in open court.

During the year ending June 30, 1959, the court promulgated 274 unanimous opinions. The remaining 116 or 30 percent were in cases on which dissenting or concurring opinions were filed.[35] Out of a total of 390 cases, 121 or 29 percent were decided by full opinions and 269 or 71 percent were decided by per curiam or memorandum decisions.[36]

All opinions are published, even the uninformative memorandum decisions. They appear in the advance sheets and bound volumes of three sets of books:

(1) the official *New York Reports;*
(2) the unofficial West Publishing Co. *New York Supplement* which contains decisions of the lower courts in the state as well; and
(3) the unofficial West Publishing Co. *Northeast Reporter,* covering not only the New York Court of Appeals, but also the supreme courts of several other nearby states.

Finality

The Court of Appeals, like most appellate courts in the United States, is besieged by petitions for rehearing. Rarely is one granted. If the court does not grant a rehearing, only two possible avenues of escape are available to the disappointed litigant.

First, he may be able to secure a further review in the Supreme Court of the United States. He can do so as of right only if the New York court has held that a federal statute violates the United States Constitution, or if it has upheld a state statute against the claim that it violates valid federal law, constitutional or otherwise. He can seek review as a matter of discretion (on the part of the United States Supreme Court) if the case involves some other federal question of controlling importance. If the case involves only questions of state law, as the overwhelming majority of cases do, the decision of the New York Court of Appeals is final.[37]

The other avenue of attack is collateral. If a civil decision of the court is called into question in another distinct proceeding, it can be challenged on the ground that the court lacked jurisdiction, but only upon that ground.[38] If a criminal proceeding is involved, however, the ground of collateral challenge is much broader—that the accused's rights under the United States Constitution were violated. The attack proceeds by way of habeas corpus in a federal district court (a single-judge trial court). This is true despite the obligation of the New York Court of Appeals to enforce federal law wherever applicable.[39]

CHAPTER FOUR

A Federal Intermediate Appellate Court

THE UNITED STATES

COURT OF APPEALS FOR

THE SECOND CIRCUIT *

General Description and Place in Judicial Hierarchy

The United States Court of Appeals for the Second Circuit is one of eleven intermediate appellate courts in the federal judicial system. It hears appeals in both civil and criminal cases from six United States district courts located in New York, Vermont, and Connecticut,[1] manned by 41 judges.[2] It has no power to review decisions of state courts.[3]

The tribunals from which appeals reach the court are trial courts of limited jurisdiction. On the criminal side, they are empowered to try only crimes against the Federal Government. There are comparatively few such, for the Federal Government, possessing power only to act within areas enumerated in the United States Constitution, lacks power to define crime generally for the nation. Consequently, most ordinary crimes—murder, robbery, rape, and the like—are defined by state legislatures and prosecuted in state courts. Federal courts deal only with offenses against the narcotics laws, immigration laws, customs laws, and other statutes within the power of Congress to enact. Because of

---

* This chapter is based in large part upon information furnished by the Hon. J. Edward Lumbard, Chief Judge of the United States Court of Appeals for the Second Circuit, to whom the author wishes to express his appreciation.

its power to regulate interstate commerce, however, the catalog of federal crimes is broader than one might expect, extending even to such matters as interstate kidnaping (the "Lindbergh law")[4] and interstate prostitution (the Mann Act).[5] Indeed, the Federal Criminal Code runs to almost 2,500 sections.[6] Nevertheless, the fact remains that federal concern with crime is far less extensive than state concern. This delimits the area of criminal jurisdiction exercised by the United States district courts.

On the civil side, the district courts enjoy a wider jurisdiction. They are empowered to try not only cases based upon federal law,[7] but also cases involving "diversity of citizenship."[8] These are cases in which the opposing parties reside in different states. In such cases, the source of the plaintiff's claim—whether state or federal law—is immaterial: a federal court will apply whichever law governs. If state law is controlling, it cannot be disregarded, whether in statutory or case-made form.[9]

Final judgments of district courts are appealable as of right.[10] Some interlocutory orders in civil cases are also appealable as a matter of right;[11] but most such orders are appealable only by permission of the court, which permission must be predicated upon a finding below that a controlling and substantial question of law is involved "upon which an immediate appeal may materially advance the ultimate termination of the litigation."[12] Relatively few interlocutory orders, whether appealable as a matter of discretion or otherwise, reach the court. Most of its time is devoted to the review of final decisions.[13]

Time and Place of Holding Court

Although authorized to sit anywhere in its circuit,[14] the court seldom sits elsewhere than in New York City. That is the source of about 90 percent of its cases, relatively few coming from Vermont, Connecticut, or the northern parts of New York State. In the courthouse at Foley Square, Manhattan, most of the judges have their regular chambers. Out of nine judges,[15] three come from outside the metropolitan area. They have chambers in United States Government buildings near their homes, as well as in the courthouse in New York, using the latter when sitting to hear arguments, and the former when writing opinions or doing other "homework."

The court sits in panels of three judges each from the end of September to the end of June. Sittings are held about 25 weeks a year in accordance with a schedule prepared by the chief judge and approved by the other judges at the beginning of the court year. The schedule determines the weeks for hearing arguments and the panels for each week. It attempts to equalize the work of all nine judges and to provide as many different combinations on panels as possible. In general, sittings are held three out of every four weeks, so that each judge will be hearing arguments for one week out of four and have the other three weeks free for work in chambers. Thus a three months' schedule might look something like this:

1st week—judges A, B, and C
2nd week—judges D, E, and F
3rd week—judges G, H, and I
4th week—no sittings
5th week—judges A, D, and G
6th week—judges B, E, and H
7th week—judges C, F, and I
8th week—no sittings
9th week—no sittings
10th week—judges A, E, and I
11th week—judges B, D, and C
12th week—judges F, G, and H
13th week—no sittings

The schedule is not published, so that the composition of the court for any given week is not generally known until after the calendar for that week has been arranged.

When a panel is sitting, it hears arguments on all five days of the week from 10:30 A.M. until about 1:30 P.M.

Only about three times a year do all nine judges sit en banc. This is likely to happen only if a fundamental divergence of opinion develops on a panel with respect to an important legal problem. The judges of that panel may then recommend to their colleagues that the case be considered en banc, or one of the parties may petition for such a hearing. If a majority of all the active judges agree that this should be done, the entire court participates in the decision. Oral argument may be scheduled before the full bench; or the case may be disposed of on the basis of the written briefs and record and the earlier consideration of the problem by the panel which originally heard the case. A good example of this procedure is provided by the case of McWeeney v. N.Y., N.H., and H. R.R., 282 F.2d 34 (1960), in which the question was whether, in a personal-injury case, the judge should instruct the jury as to the effect of federal income taxes on an award of damages. The panel hearing the case originally split two to one and then the entire court reconsidered the case on the papers alone. (There was still a dissent.)

On special occasions, a panel of the court may be convened during the summer to hear an emergency case. If so, it will sit only long enough to hear that case. This is not likely to happen more than two or three times during a summer.

Personnel

Judges are appointed by the President with the advice and consent of the Senate.[16] Some have previous judicial experience; others do not. They serve for life (technically "during good behavior") and are not subject to mandatory retirement at any age. However, when a judge, having served 10 years, reaches the age of 70, or, having served 15 years, reaches the age of 65, he can voluntarily retire. If he does so, he continues to receive full salary for life, even to the point of receiving any increase in salary which might be granted by Congress.[17] The present salary is $25,500 per year.[18]

Upon retirement, a judge becomes known as a senior judge and he may continue to function as a member of the court to the extent that he and the active judges agree. By manifesting a willingness to serve on a regular, albeit limited basis, he can retain his chambers, his law clerk, and his secretary. Because of inadequate regular manpower until the 1961 increase in the number of judges, the court has relied heavily on the services of senior judges in the last few years.[19] It has also availed itself of the services of judges from other circuits and district judges specially assigned.

The administrative head of the court is the chief judge. He attains that position by virtue of his seniority in service on the court, and retains the post until reaching the age of 70.[20] Thereafter he can continue as a regular member of the court, but not as chief judge.

By virtue of seniority, the chief judge presides over any panel on which he sits and he assigns the writing of opinions in the cases so heard. Otherwise, he operates like any of his colleagues, carrying the same share of judicial work as falls to them. In addition, however, he carries the burden of administrative and housekeeping chores for the court; and, as chief judge for the entire circuit, head of the judicial council for the circuit, and a member of the Judicial Conference of the United States, he plays an important role in the administration of the whole federal judicial system. The judicial council, which consists of the nine active circuit judges, is empowered to "make all necessary orders for the effective and expeditious administration of the business of the courts within the circuit." [21] The Judicial Conference, which consists of key federal judges from all over the nation, is authorized to "make a comprehensive survey of the condition of business in the courts of the United States and prepare plans for the assignment of judges to or from circuits or districts where necessary, and shall submit suggestions to the various courts, in the interest of uniformity and expedition of business." [22]

Each judge has the help of a law clerk and a secretary, chosen by himself. The law clerks are typically recent graduates of law schools, replaced each year. They receive salaries of $6,435 per year.

Volume and Scope of Work

During the year ending June 30, 1961, the court heard 365 appeals, rendering 259 regular opinions and 106 per curiam opinions. In addition, 76 dissenting and concurring opinions were filed.[23]

During this period, there were only six regular members of the court, each of whom participated, on the average, in 140 cases during the year.[24] With three new judges, the caseload should be eased. However, the effect of the increase in manpower may be less drastic than anticipated, for two reasons: (1) with many new district judges in the circuit, the number of appeals may be expected to increase; and (2) fewer calls for help are likely to be made upon senior and specially assigned judges.

This volume of cases is greater than that of most other United States Courts of Appeals.[25] It is considerably less, however, than the volume of work handled by the Appellate Division of the New York Supreme Court, First Department.[26]

The ratio of appeals to trials is high. In the year ending June 30, 1960, about 200 criminal and 677 civil cases were tried in all of the district courts comprising the Second Circuit. (The great majority of all criminal cases resulted in pleas of guilty and the great majority of civil cases were settled.) In the same year, the Court of Appeals disposed of 57 criminal appeals and 305 civil appeals.[27] Some of the civil appeals, it should be noted, were from judgments rendered without trial, as upon motions to dismiss or for summary judgment.

As for the scope of review, the court considers questions of fact as well as questions of law. It will not, however, substitute its judgment for the verdict of a jury (or the finding of an administrative agency), but will limit itself to inquiring whether there is substantial evidence to support it. When reviewing cases tried by a judge alone, it will accord respect to his superior opportunity to determine the credibility of witnesses and will ordinarily limit itself to reviewing the inferences and value judgments [28] made by him. It will not reverse unless it concludes that the findings of the district judge were "clearly erroneous." [29]

The court follows the usual American pattern in interpreting statutes (using legislative history when available), in overruling its own precedents when they are deemed to have outlived their usefulness, and in granting new trials in criminal as well as civil cases.

In addition to appeals, the court disposes of over 500 motions a year.[30] Almost all of these pertain to pending appeals—applications for bail in criminal cases, for extensions of time, for permission to dispense with the printing of briefs, and the like. They are heard on any Monday when the court is sitting and seldom consume more than an hour or an hour and a half of the court's time. Most are decided from the bench after a few minutes of explanation by counsel.

Documents on Appeal

After the entry of judgment in the district court, the defendant in a criminal case, or any party aggrieved in a civil case, may serve on all other parties and file with the district court a notice of appeal.[31] This document contains little information beyond the fact that an appeal is being taken. In particular, it gives no indication of the alleged errors which will be relied upon as the basis for reversal or modification of the decision below.[32] That is left to the brief of the appellant.

A streamlined record of what transpired in the trial court will have to be presented to the Court of Appeals, but that can be done most economically and efficiently after the points to be argued on appeal have become clarified. Consequently, the first order of business for the appellant is to prepare his brief.

The brief is a written argument, describing the nature of the case, the questions raised on appeal, the proceedings out of which they arose, and the reasons urged for reversal or modification of the judgment below. Authorities, in the form of statutes, decisions, and commentaries, are cited and discussed.[33] The brief may not exceed 50 pages in length without special leave (which is almost always granted if asked), and it must be served upon the appellee and filed in the court within 30 days after the record is filed.[34]

The record, properly speaking, is the collection of original papers used in the trial court plus the transcript of testimony.[35]

It is transmitted by the clerk of the trial court to the appellate court within 40 days of the filing of the notice of appeal.[36] Adding this time to the time allowed for the filing of the first brief, it can be seen that the appellant normally has 70 days after taking an appeal to prepare, serve, and file his brief.

Accompanying the appellant's brief and sometimes bound with it into a single volume is an appendix, reproducing such portions of the record as are relevant to the questions raised on appeal. Included are the formal papers in the case—pleadings, verdict, judgment, and the like—plus such exhibits and such parts of the stenographic transcript of the evidence as may be necessary to an understanding of the appeal.[37] This is a supporting reference type document. The brief describes the proceedings and contains citations to the appendix, wherein the appellate judges may verify for themselves the happenings described.

Upon being served with a copy of the appellant's brief, the appellee prepares his brief. Ordinarily, this is a purely defensive argument intended to convince the court that the judgment below was correct and should be affirmed. It, too, cites and discusses authorities, and gives the appellee's version of the facts. The appellee may also submit an appendix to his own brief, reproducing additional parts of the record. If, however, his arguments can be predicated on the record as reproduced in the appendix to the appellant's brief, there is no need for the appellee to file his own appendix.[38] He will merely cite the appellant's appendix. The appellee's brief, like the appellant's, is limited to 50 pages in length. It must be served and filed within 20 days after the filing of the appellant's brief.[39] Within 15 additional days, the appellant, if so disposed, may file a reply brief, limited to 20 pages in length.[40]

All briefs and appendices are required to be printed,[41] unless the court allows the appeal to be prosecuted on papers reproduced in a less expensive manner, as by typewriting.[42] Applications to dispense with printing are seldom refused. Fifteen copies of each brief and 24 copies of each appendix are required to be filed, allowing one for each judge—even if the court should sit en banc— as well as several to be distributed to law libraries.[43]

The total time consumed in the preparation, service, and

filing of briefs in the average case need not exceed two months. To this must be added the time allowed for taking an appeal and for the clerk of the district court to transmit the original record to the appellate court. A complete time schedule in a civil case up to this point might therefore look something like this:

30 days—filing notice of appeal
40 days—transmittal of original record
30 days—filing of appellant's brief
20 days—filing of appellee's brief
15 days—filing of reply brief

TOTAL 135 days

Usually, however, more time is taken. Opposing counsel are likely to be indulgent toward each other with respect to deadlines, and the court itself often extends time for good cause shown. Hence, in the average case, about seven months are likely to elapse between judgment in the court below and the filing of the last brief.

Sometimes, on the other hand, the procedure is expedited. In any emergency situation, the court will work out with counsel a special schedule for the accelerated serving and filing of papers.

Oral Argument

Very shortly after the last brief is filed, a case comes on for oral argument.[44] Almost all cases are argued, less than two percent being submitted on the briefs. Most members of the court find oral argument helpful, however much they might hope for an improvement in its quality.

At the beginning of a day's hearing, the presiding judge knows approximately how much time is going to be consumed in each case. This has been ascertained previously by the clerk of the court. The rules permit a maximum of 45 minutes for each side without special leave of the court obtained in advance, but ordinarily a lawyer is expected to ask for no more than 20 minutes. If he wants more time, he must give reasons which satisfy the judge who will preside. Communications between the court and counsel on this subject are carried on by mail in advance of the time for argument.

On the basis of these communications, the clerk prepares the list of cases for each day, scheduling as many as will occupy the time of the panel for three hours. Ordinarily, three or four cases a day are scheduled. Not infrequently, counsel use less time than has been allotted them.

The judges may or may not have read the briefs in advance. The tendency today is strongly toward reading them in advance. Since arguments are scheduled for certain dates,[45] a judge can read them with some assurance that he will not have forgotten them by the time he hears argument in the case. When hearing argument, no judge knows whether he will be called upon to write an opinion in the case. Usually that is not decided until the conference the following week.

A considerable amount of time may be consumed by questions from the court. Whether such time counts against the time allotted to counsel is a question on which there is no hard and fast rule; the presiding judge exercises his discretion case by case. Extended reading by counsel during the course of argument is strongly disapproved. The judges much prefer to study for themselves any material that exists in written form in order to save time.

Summary Dispositions

At the conclusion of all arguments for one day, the judges meet informally (sometimes while walking away from the courtroom, sometimes while having lunch) to determine if any of the cases just heard are susceptible of easy and quick disposition. If there are any such cases in the view of the entire panel, the presiding judge assigns to himself or either of his two colleagues the preparation of per curiam opinions. These opinions are expected to be drafted and circulated within a few days. About 25 percent of the cases are disposed of in this manner.

On rare occasions, the judges decide a case from the bench. This happens only if all of them are thoroughly satisfied after hearing the appellant that the judgment below should be affirmed without modification. In that case they may decline to hear the appellee and announce their decision forthwith (but not their reasons, which presumably will follow a week or two hence in the form of a per curiam opinion). It might be added that the judges are not likely to proceed in this manner unless they have studied the briefs in advance; they are hesitant to rely too heavily on oral argument alone.

Until recently, very few cases were decided from the bench—only about five per year. In 1961–62, however, the number rose sharply to eighteen. This may be attributable, at least in part, to the Anglo-American interchange described in Chapter One. Chief Judge Lumbard was a member of the American team which observed English appellate courts disposing of the great majority of their cases orally (and extemporaneously) immediately upon the close of oral argument.

Preparation for Conference

With respect to any case not disposed of in a manner already described, the court follows what is believed to be a unique practice among American appellate courts: each judge on the panel prepares a written memorandum of his views. It is understood by all concerned that the conclusions expressed are tentative and subject to change as a result of further consideration.

The preparation of these memoranda requires independent study by every judge of every case in which he participates, and provides as good an antidote as any yet devised against the evil of "one-man opinions." Each judge of the court is placed in approximately the same position as the "reporting" judge on the New York Court of Appeals or the New York Appellate Division, First Department.

As for the extent to which each judge must study the briefs, appendices, and authorities cited, that depends upon the same considerations which motivate any judge in doing preliminary work on an opinion. That is what in substance each judge is doing when he prepares his memorandum, which may run in length anywhere from a paragraph to eight or ten pages. The memoranda are exchanged between the judges of the panel prior to the time of their conference.

The Conference

During the week following a week of argument, the judges meet in conference at a time mutually convenient to them. The purpose is to discuss the cases not yet disposed of by per curiam opinions. Since the memoranda on these cases have been circulated in advance, the issues to be resolved are well understood by all concerned. This makes for an efficient and relatively short (normally two to three hours) conference.

In an average conference, there are 12 to 15 cases to be considered. They are discussed one by one, with the senior judge, who presided at the argument, leading the discussion. The group is so small, however, that great informality prevails, with each judge presenting his views as extensively as he wishes. Cases are discussed to the extent necessary to clarify the views of all judges. It is not uncommon at this time for one of them to switch his position and embrace a view contrary to that expressed by him earlier in his own memorandum on the case.

When a conclusion is reached, the presiding judge assigns the writing of the opinion for the court, taking into account the desires of his colleagues and the burdens of opinion-writing already resting upon them. There is no automatic rotation system such as prevails in the appellate courts of New York.

Opinions

Opinions are written in all cases, although as already indicated, some take the per curiam form. The per curiam opinions are usually unanimous affirmances where no significant questions of law are involved. Occasionally, however, they are used where the judges are agreed upon the result but not the reasons. If so, the reasons may be stated in such general form that they are not unpalatable to any of the participating judges.

Typically a per curiam opinion runs to only a page or two in length. Occasionally, it is compressed into a single brief paragraph. An ordinary opinion runs at least three pages in length, sometimes as much as 15, 20, or more pages.

The task of drafting an opinion is made easier by what has preceded it—the conference, the informal discussions, and the exchange of memoranda between the judges. Indeed, something approaching a first rough draft is already in existence in the form of three memoranda. In other words, something is already down on paper—a great boon to any writer, even though the heavy job of draftsmanship lies ahead. Further study of the briefs and records and further research will almost always be necessary; but at least the lines of inquiry have been defined. Informal conferences between the judges either in person or by telephone may also be held. At this stage of opinion-writing as well as at the earlier stage of preparing memoranda, the judge has the assistance of his law clerk.

Since the court produces about 106 per curiam and 259 signed opinions a year, the annual average for each of the nine judges now on the court can be expected to be about 12 per curiam and 29 signed opinions. From October through June, this should work out to about one regular opinion a week and one per curiam every other week. Dissenting and concurring opinions are extra and not included in these estimates. (In recent years, when the court had only six regular members, all the judges worked on opinions during much of the summer as well as during the court year.)

When a judge has put an opinion for the court into shape that satisfies himself, he circulates copies to his colleagues. They offer suggestions freely, either in person, by telephone, or by written notes, in an effort to reach agreement. Sometimes an opinion is redrafted several times in order to produce the desired result with reasons satisfactory to all or a majority of the judges concerned. In about 85 percent of the cases, a single opinion is filed.

In the remaining 15 percent, dissenting or concurring opinions are filed. When a judge cannot go along with his colleagues after studying the draft proposed for the opinion of the court, he decides for himself whether he will draft a separate opinion. If he decides to do so, he circulates copies to his colleagues. Sometimes they change their views, so that what started out to be a dissenting opinion turns out to be the opinion of the court. It may even be unanimous. Or the opposite may happen: the majority judges may redraft their opinion in such a way that the dissenting judge is convinced.

Once the judges have reached a unanimous opinion, or, where there is disagreement, when they have reached a conclusion as to which opinion expresses the majority view, the next step is to promulgate the decision. No formality attaches to this step. Opinions are not read aloud or even announced in open court, but are made public by being filed with the clerk. He causes them to be printed as "slip opinions"—i.e., separate documents—and forthwith distributes copies to the parties concerned, all judges in the Second Circuit, all circuit judges in other circuits, selected libraries and law schools, and the West Publishing Company. That company reprints all opinions, which then appear both in the advance sheets and bound volumes of a set of books known as the *Federal 2nd Reports.*

The entire process of reaching a final decision after oral argument takes, on the average, about seven weeks.[46] Adding this to the time spent in reaching oral argument (seven months, on the average), it will be seen that the total average time elapsing between trial court decision and appellate court decision is about nine months.

Finality

Rehearings are requested in about half the cases decided. The losing party within 15 days submits a printed petition setting forth the reasons why he thinks the court has erred.[47] Copies are distributed to the three judges who heard the case and they indicate their votes in writing. If the petition asks a rehearing en banc (as often happens), copies then go to the remaining six judges, who likewise vote in writing to grant or deny the petition.

Very few petitions for rehearing are granted. Occasionally, however, as the result of a petition, the language of an opinion will be changed to eliminate an ambiguity or correct a misstatement. If a rehearing is granted, the court reconsiders the case on the papers alone, and does not hear oral argument. Occasionally, it reverses its position upon such reconsideration.

While petitions for rehearing impose a burden upon the court, consuming many hours of judge-time during the course of a year, they have the advantage of allowing the judges a final occasion to reflect upon the cases under consideration. They have already had many opportunities to deliberate and to change their minds—during oral argument, while drafting memoranda, in conference, and while drafting opinions—and the petition for rehearing presents still another opportunity to avoid error.

Decisions of the court are subject to review in the United States Supreme Court. A few go there as a matter of right, but most only as a matter of discretion exercised by that Court.[48] Whether discretionary or not, few cases go beyond the United States Court of Appeals for the Second Circuit. In the year ending June 30, 1960, when the court decided 362 cases, only 9 cases from the Second Circuit (some of which doubtless came from previous years) were being reviewed on the merits in the Supreme Court.[49] In the next year, only 14 petitions for certiorari out of 154 were granted. In short, less than 5 percent of the cases are reviewed by the Supreme Court.

CHAPTER FIVE

The Highest Tribunal

THE SUPREME COURT

OF THE UNITED STATES *

General Description and Place in Judicial Hierarchy

The United States lacks a unified national system of courts. Instead, 51 systems are in operation, one for each of the 50 states and another for the Federal Government.[1] In this complicated structure, the Supreme Court occupies a unique position. It is not only the highest federal court, but also possesses power to review decisions of the highest courts of the various states insofar as they rest upon determinations of federal questions.[2] It is thus the ultimate arbiter of federal law and the tying force that binds together all the courts of the nation.

Criminal as well as civil appeals reach the Court. Most cases have already been through at least one stage of appellate review—either in one of the fifty state supreme courts [3] or one of the eleven federal Courts of Appeals. A few, however, come directly from trial courts. In some special situations (for example, where, in a civil action to which the Federal Government is a party, an act of Congress has been held unconstitutional), a direct appeal may be taken from a United States district court.[4] Similarly, direct review of the decision of a lower state court is possible in exceptional circumstances. In 1960, a case of this kind arose. A man was con-

---

* © 1962 British Institute of International and Comparative Law. The writer is much indebted to the Hon. William J. Brennan, Jr., Associate Justice of the Supreme Court, for having read and commented upon this paper.

victed of loitering and disorderly conduct in a police court of Louisville, Kentucky, and fined $10.00. He claimed that the charges against him were "so totally devoid of evidentiary support as to render his conviction unconstitutional under the due process clause of the Fourteenth Amendment." Under the state statutes, however, there was no court to which he could appeal in so seemingly trivial a case. In these circumstances, the United States Supreme Court granted review of the case and reversed the conviction.[5]

Such situations are very unusual. About 60 percent of the cases heard on the merits by the Supreme Court come from the United States Courts of Appeal; about 20 percent from state supreme courts; and most of the remainder from United States district courts.[6]

Specialization of Function

A state case can reach the Court only if it involves a question of federal law of controlling importance. State courts are required to apply federal law wherever it is applicable,[7] but since the scope of such law is limited,[8] relatively few of their cases are affected by it. Most of them involve torts, contracts, real property, and other areas of private law where there is no federal legislation and where, moreover, no federal constitutional question is raised. With such cases, the United States Supreme Court has no concern, for it recognizes that "there is no general federal common law" and that on questions of state law, case-made or statutory, state courts have the final word.[9]

In a relatively small proportion of state cases, federal questions are present. These may or may not be controlling. Thus a litigant might challenge a state statute as being in conflict with both the state constitution and the federal constitution. If the highest court of the state invalidated the statute on the ground that it violated the state constitution or on the ground that it violated both constitutions, the United States Supreme Court would have no interest in the case. The state ground of decision would be adequate to support it, and the federal question would have become moot.[10] If, on the other hand, the state court upheld the statute under the state constitution but invalidated it under the federal constitution, the case would be appropriate for review in the United States Supreme Court. The federal ground of decision, in other words, would be controlling. Similarly if a claim predicated upon a federal statute (like the Federal Employers' Liability Act) were brought in a state court and if the highest appellate court in the state interpreted the statute in such a way as to bar the claim, and if that were the sole basis for its decision, the case would present an appropriate question for review in the Supreme Court of the United States. In short, insofar as its cases come from state courts, the Supreme Court is a specialized tribunal: it handles only federal questions.

Insofar as its cases come from the lower federal courts, the situation is not much different. Potentially all cases in federal courts are eligible for ultimate review in the Supreme Court, regardless of the questions litigated. Nevertheless, the jurisdiction of these courts is such as to ensure that the only questions they yield for review are federal questions. The only criminal cases they handle are those involving violations of the federal criminal statutes; and about half their civil cases arise under the Constitution, laws, or treaties of the United States. It is only in the remaining half of the civil cases that nonfederal questions might be expected to develop. These are cases based solely upon diversity of citizenship. Insofar as such cases involve incidentally questions of federal law (the right to trial by jury under the Seventh Amendment to the Constitution, for example), they are on a par with the cases already discussed. Insofar as they involve questions of state law, such questions are important to decision in the lower federal courts, but they are of little concern to the Supreme Court. There is no dispute as to the general proposition that on such questions state decisions and state statutes are controlling, so that the only problem for the Supreme Court is to see that the lower federal courts respect state sources of decision.

The conclusion must be, therefore, that in all of its cases—those coming from federal courts as well as those coming from state courts—the Supreme Court is a specialized tribunal, handling only federal questions. This is not to suggest that the Court's jurisdiction is narrow or unimportant—far from it—but only that it is limited, allowing the justices to become experts in matters of national concern. So great is their specialization in some areas— constitutional law, for example—that they are sometimes more familiar with the law governing a particular case at the outset of argument than the lawyers who have briefed it.[11] In other areas of federal law with which they deal less frequently—taxes, patents, admiralty matters, and the like—they tend to be like any other appellate judges: generally familiar, but not expert.

Discretionary Review

Today relatively few cases reach the Supreme Court as a matter of right. At one time many did, but the press of business was such that Congress, by a series of statutes culminating in the Judiciary Act of 1925,[12] gave the Court a very large measure of control over its own docket. The objective was to allow it to concentrate its energies on crucial questions of nationwide concern. Today, as a consequence, most cases reach the Court only by its permission.

CERTIORARI

Discretionary review is exercised by means of "writs of certiorari." [13] A litigant seeking review serves on the other parties and files wtih the Court a petition for certiorari, in which he seeks not so much to show that an error was committed below as to demonstrate that the question presented is one of general interest, deserving consideration by the highest tribunal of the land. The Court has defined the kinds of cases it considers appropriate in these words:

1. A review on writ of certiorari is not a matter of right, but of sound judicial discretion, and will be granted only where there are special and important reasons therefor. The following, while neither controlling nor fully measuring the court's discretion, indicate the character of reasons which will be considered.

(a) Where a state court has decided a federal question of substance not theretofore determined by this court, or has decided it in a way probably not in accord with applicable decisions of this court.

(b) Where a court of appeals has rendered a decision in conflict with the decision of another court of appeals on the same matter; or has decided an important state or territorial question in a way in conflict with applicable state or territorial law; or has decided an important question of federal law which has not been, but should be, settled by this court; or has decided a federal question in a way in conflict with applicable decisions of this court; or has so far departed from the accepted and usual course of judicial proceedings, or so far sanctioned such a departure by a lower court, as to call for an exercise of this court's power of supervision.

2. The same general considerations outlined above will control in respect of petitions for writs of certiorari to review judgments of the Court of Claims, of the Court of Customs and Patent Appeals, or of any other court whose determinations are by law reviewable on writ of certiorari.[14]

The same principles have been expressed frequently and in various forms by many members of the Court on many occasions.[15] Nevertheless, hundreds of petitions are filed each year which can hardly be described as better than frivolous in their attempts to justify review.

All petitions, whether meritorious or otherwise, some 1,300 in number,[16] must be screened to discover the relatively few cases which are worthy of plenary consideration. Each of the nine Justices participates in the process, voting on every application. Authority is not delegated to any one Justice or to any committee, panel, or division of Justices, nor is it shifted to nonjudicial personnel.

About half the petitions are in printed form, allowing a copy for each Justice. The other half are in forma pauperis and consist of a single typewritten or handwritten copy (often an almost illiterate and illegible product from the inmate of some prison), which must be either circulated from one Justice to another or considered on the basis of excerpts extracted from it and distributed to all.[17]

In addition to the petitions, there may be, and usually are, briefs in opposition to be considered, and sometimes even records on appeal as used in the courts below.

On the basis of their study of these documents, the Justices vote at their conference (to be described later). If four of them favor granting certiorari, that becomes the ruling of the Court; if less than four are in favor, the petition is denied.[18] The denial of a petition does not signify that the Court approves the decision below, but only that it does not regard the case as being appropriate for plenary consideration.[19]

Despite the fact that the Justices generally avoid any attempt to deal with the merits in passing upon petitions for certiorari, sometimes that is impossible: an error may be glaringly clear. Occasionally, therefore, the Court, in the process of granting certiorari, will simultaneously and summarily—without receiving briefs on the merits or hearing argument—reverse the decision below.[20]

The votes of the Justices in granting or denying certiorari and the reasons behind them are not ordinarily revealed. Sometimes, however, sharp differences of opinion come to light with respect to the specific application of the general principles discussed above. A particular focus of controversy has been the granting of certiorari to review the sufficiency of evidence in jury-tried cases. Some members of the Court believe that such review is necessary to vindicate the constitutional right to trial by jury and to ensure compliance with federal substantive rights embodied in statutes like the Federal Employers' Liability Act; others that it is a waste of the Court's time,[21] frustrating its main job of "expounding and stabilizing principles of law" for the national benefit.[22]

APPEALS

A few cases reach the Court as of right. These are called appeals, and they lie in the following circumstances:

From a United States Court of Appeals if a party is relying on a state statute held to be invalid "as repugnant to the Constitution, treaties or laws of the United States." [23]

From a state court if its decision is against the validity of a treaty or statute of the United States; or if it upholds a state statute against the contention that it is repugnant to the Constitution, treaties or laws of the United States.[24]

Despite the mandatory character of the Court's jurisdiction in these cases, it screens them in much the same way it screens petitions for certiorari. A litigant taking an appeal is required to file not only a notice of appeal, but also a "statement of jurisdiction" showing why the case belongs in the Supreme Court.[25] The appellee thereupon may file a motion to dismiss or a motion to affirm.[26] Then the Court, operating by the individual vote of all nine Justices and following the "rule of four" [27] decides whether the case should stay. It may dismiss the appeal not only because technical grounds of jurisdiction are lacking, but also "for want of a substantial federal question." Another disposition it can and occasionally does make is to summarily affirm or reverse the decision below without hearing oral argument or receiving briefs on the merits.

Out of 1,787 cases presented to the Court during the year ended June 30, 1959, both by way of appeal and by way of petition for certiorari, only 126 were heard on oral argument. The remainder were disposed of on papers alone—very few on the merits, most only by refusal of the Court to entertain jurisdiction.[28]

Personnel

The Court consists of a Chief Justice and eight Associate Justices, all appointed by the President with the advice and consent of the Senate.[29] In making appointments, Presidents traditionally have been guided not only by considerations of fitness for office, but also by such considerations as geographical balance, religious background, and political affiliation. While such factors have no bearing on professional competency, they are relevant to the goal of securing representation of a fair cross section of the American community on what is recognized as a vital policy-making body for the nation.[30] Some of the present Justices have had previous judicial experience; others have not. Some come from academic halls, some from political careers, some from private practice.

The Justices have life tenure [31] and are not subject to mandatory retirement at any age. They may voluntarily retire, however, upon reaching the age of 70, having served 10 years, or at the age of 65, having served 15 years.[32] They receive salaries of $35,000 per year, except for the Chief Justice, who receives $35,500.[33]

The Chief Justice is the administrative head of the Court. In this capacity, he has the important duty of presiding over conferences of the Justices, and of assigning the writing of opinions for the Court when he votes with the majority. Beyond the Court itself, he is charged with important responsibilities in the total administration of the federal court system. He is chairman of the Judicial Conference of the United States, a policy-making body composed of the Chief Judges of the 11 Courts of Appeals and other key federal judges,[34] and he supervises, unofficially but in fact, the operations of the Administrative Office of the United States Courts.[35]

Each Associate Justice is entitled to the assistance of two law clerks; the Chief Justice has three. All of them are recent law school graduates, chosen by the Justices individually, and normally replaced each year. Most of them receive salaries of $6,616.50 per annum.

Time and Place of Holding Court

The Court sits only in Washington, D.C.[36] Since its cases originate in all parts of the nation, including Hawaii and Alaska, lawyers occasionally have to travel as much as 5–6,000 miles to be heard. Despite the time and expense involved, they rarely submit on their briefs alone or retain special counsel for argument from Washington or the nearby cities of New York, Philadelphia, or Baltimore. Twenty-five or thirty years ago there was what might be called a specialized Supreme Court bar, but it seems to have gone out of existence with the changing character of the cases brought before the Court (away from an emphasis on commercial problems toward an emphasis on civil rights problems).

Sittings are held from the first Monday in October to the middle of June, in accordance with a schedule prepared by the Chief Justice at the beginning of each Court year. Out of about 36 weeks available, 16 are used for hearing arguments, with the Court sitting for two weeks, then recessing for two or three, then sitting for two, recessing for two or three, and so on. During the weeks of sitting, Mondays, Tuesdays, Wednesdays, and Thursdays are devoted to hearing arguments from 10:00 A.M. to 2:30 P.M. On Mondays, part of the time—but rarely more than an hour—may be devoted to the announcement of decisions in cases previously heard, with each Justice reading aloud the opinions prepared by him or summaries thereof. Fridays preceding Mondays when decisions are so announced are devoted to conferences between the Justices, as are also Fridays during weeks when arguments are heard.

Volume, Scope, and Nature of Work

The volume of work has already been indicated in the figures showing the number of applications made to the Court for review and the number of cases accepted by it for plenary consideration. Each application entails the expenditure of time on the part of each Justice in studying the papers and participating in conference. Each case fully heard entails a far greater expenditure of time in deciding on the merits. The Court sits and acts only en banc, and every decision it makes—whether to grant review, whether to reverse, modify, or affirm, or whether to grant a rehearing—represents the collective judgment of nine men. This presents internal problems far more difficult than are encountered in a court which consists of three, five, or seven judges, or which operates in small panels or divisions.

Despite heavy pressures of time and sharp criticism of its practice, the Court reviews determinations of fact as well as determinations of law. Such questions arise sometimes from the contention that a litigant's constitutional right to trial by jury is being denied by a lower federal court's direction of a verdict,[37] and sometimes from the contention that a litigant's rights under federal substantive law are being frustrated by a lower state or federal court's direction of a verdict.[38] Under either contention, the Supreme Court's jurisdiction to decide federal questions is properly invoked, provided—and this is the focus of the dispute over the Court's taking such cases—that the time can be spared from the consideration of allegedly more important federal questions.

Deciding questions of law, however, is the main occupation of the Court. In dealing with such questions, it tends to set the pattern for American appellate review generally. Three aspects of the pattern are especially noteworthy:

1. In construing statutes, the Court makes use of legislative history. Such history is more abundantly available in connection with Congressional enactments—the source of most of the Court's problems—than in connection with most state legislation. The Court takes full advantage of it, believing, as it does, that the purpose of a statute is as important as its language.

2. The Court overrules its own prior decisions when it concludes that they have outlived their usefulness. In part, this is explained by the special subject matter of many of them—constitutional law. Erroneous or outmoded decisions in this area are not subject to legislative correction. They can be cured only by the very cumbersome process of constitutional amendment or by corrective action on the part of the Court itself.

The Court's willingness to overrule precedents, however, is not confined to constitutional decisions. It extends to other areas of law, even to the extent that the Court is willing to overrule, on nonconstitutional grounds, prior decisions interpreting statutes. Thus in Nye v. United States,[39] Mr. Justice Douglas, speaking for the Court, said:

> We are dealing here only with a problem of statutory construction, not with a question as to the constitutionally permissible scope of the contempt power. But that is no reason why we should adhere to the construction adopted by Toledo Newspaper Co. v. United States, supra, and leave to Congress the task of delimiting the statute as thus interpreted.

3. The Court is frank in recognizing its lawmaking function. Its opinions are replete with discussions of social policy. It offers no pretense that all of its decisions are derived only by logical deduction from preexisting legal rules. Thus, in Green v. United States,[40] Mr. Justice Black, dissenting, said:

Ordinarily it is sound policy to adhere to prior decisions but this practice has quite properly never been a blind, inflexible rule. Courts are not omniscient. Like every other human agency, they too can profit from trial and error, from experience and reflection. As others have demonstrated, the principle commonly referred to as stare decisis has never been thought to extend so far as to prevent the courts from correcting their own errors. Accordingly, this Court has time and time again from the very beginning reconsidered the merits of its earlier decisions even though they claimed great longevity and repeated reaffirmation. See, e.g., Erie Railroad Co. v. Tompkins, 304 U.S. 64, 58 S.Ct. 817, 82 L.Ed. 1188; Graves v. People of State of New York ex rel. O'Keefe, 306 U.S. 466, 59 S.Ct. 595, 83 L.Ed. 927; Nye v. United States, 313 U.S. 33, 61 S.Ct. 810, 85 L.Ed. 1172. Indeed, the Court has a special responsibility where questions of constitutional law are involved to review its decisions from time to time and where compelling reasons present themselves to refuse to follow erroneous precedents; otherwise its mistakes in interpreting the Constitution are extremely difficult to alleviate and needlessly so. See Burnet v. Coronado Oil & Gas Co., 285 U.S. 393, 405; 52 S.Ct. 443, 446; 76 L.Ed. 815 (Brandeis, J., dissenting); Douglas, Stare Decisis, 49 Col. L. Rev. 735.

Mr. Justice Frankfurter, concurring with the majority, said:

To be sure, it is never too late for this Court to correct a misconception in an occasional decision, even on a rare occasion to change a rule of law that may have long persisted but also have long been questioned and only fluctuatingly applied. To say that everybody on the Court has been wrong for 150 years and that that which has been deemed part of the bone and sinew of the law should now be extirpated is quite another thing. Decision-making is not a mechanical process, but neither is this Court an originating lawmaker. The admonition of Mr. Justice Brandeis that we are not a third branch of the Legislature should never be disregarded. Congress has seen fit from time to time to qualify the power of summary punishment for contempt that it gave the federal courts in 1789 by requiring in explicitly defined situations that a jury be associated with the court in determining whether there has been a contempt. See, e.g., 18 U.S.C. § 3691, 18 U.S.C.A. § 3691; Civil Rights Act of 1957, 71 Stat. 634, 638, 42 U.S.C. § 1995, 42 U.S.C.A. § 1995. It is for Congress to extend this participation of the jury, whenever it sees fit to do so, to other instances of the exercise of the power to punish for contempt. It is not for this Court to fashion a wholly novel constitutional doctrine that would require such participation whatever Congress may think on the matter, and in the teeth of an unbroken legislative and judicial history from the foundation of the Nation.

The difference between them, it will be noted, is not on the general principle involved, but on its application to a particular case.

The Court's attitude is explained in part by the peculiar nature of constitutional law, its special concern. Constitutional provisions are notoriously uninformative: "due process of law," "necessary and proper," "interstate commerce," and like phrases gain specific content only in decisions interpreting and applying them to particular situations.

Nevertheless the Court's avowal of its lawmaking role is not limited to constitutional adjudication. It extends as well into the field of statutory interpretation, where, in dealing with such concepts as "combinations in restraint of trade," the Court acknowledges that statutes mean only what it says they mean.

Thus in Appalachian Coals Inc. v. U.S.,[41] Mr. Chief Justice Hughes said:

The purpose of the Sherman Anti-Trust Act is to prevent undue restraints of interstate commerce, to maintain its appropriate freedom in the public interest, to afford protection from the subversive or coercive influences of monopolistic endeavor. As a charter of freedom, the Act has a generality and adaptability comparable to that found to be desirable in constitutional provisions. It does not go into detailed definitions which might either work injury to legitimate enterprise or through particularization defeat its purposes by providing loopholes for escape. The restrictions the Act imposes are not mechanical or artificial. Its general phrases, interpreted to attain its fundamental objects, set up the essential standard of reasonableness. They call for vigilance in the detection and frustration of all efforts unduly to restrain the free course of interstate commerce, but they do not seek to establish a mere delusive liberty either by making impossible the normal and fair expansion of that commerce or the adoption of reasonable measures to protect it from injurious and destructive practices and to promote competition upon a sound basis. . . .

Documents

Some of the documents submitted to the Court have already been mentioned: the petition for certiorari and the brief in opposition; or, in the case of an appeal, the statement of jurisdiction and the motion to dismiss or to affirm.

Once a case has been accepted for plenary consideration, further papers are required. The first, due within 20 days, is a designation by the appellant (hereafter this term is used to denote the petitioner for a writ of certiorari as well as one who takes an appeal) of the parts of the record which he considers necessary for the Court's consideration of the questions presented.[42] Within 10 more days, the other side may designate additional parts of the record as necessary for this purpose.[43] On the basis of these designations, the clerk of the Court arranges for printing 40 copies of the record. The expense of printing, which in one recent case came to almost $100,000, must be paid in advance by the appellant. If, however, he is in a position to furnish 40 printed copies of the record used in the court below, it becomes necessary to freshly print only such additions as will show the proceedings in that court and the opinions there rendered. If the Court allows review in forma pauperis, the cost of printing is borne by the government.[44] When the printing is completed, five copies of the finished product are distributed to counsel for each side, and the remaining 30 copies retained for the use of the Court.[45]

Thereafter the parties serve and file their briefs. The appellant has 30 days after receiving the printed record within which to serve and file his brief; and the appellee has 30 days after receiving the appellant's brief to serve and file his own. If the appellant wishes to submit a reply, he may do so at any time up to the time of oral argument. All briefs are required to be printed. While no arbitrary limits are placed upon their length,[46] verbose briefs are regarded with disfavor by the Court.

The total time schedule in a certiorari case coming from a state court up to this point might look something like this if no postponements of time were granted:

    90 days—filing petition for certiorari [47]
    30 days—brief in opposition [48]
    30 days—grant of petition by court
    20 days—filing designation of parts of record to be printed
    10 days—cross designation by other side
    15 days—printed record complete
    30 days—petitioner's brief on the merits
    30 days—appellee's brief on the merits
TOTAL   255 days

The time would be less if the case came from a lower federal court, mainly because only 30 days rather than 90 would be allowed for filing the initial application for review.[49]

Oral Argument

Within about two weeks after the appellee's brief has been filed,[50] a case comes before the Court for oral argument. It could be submitted on the briefs alone, but that seldom happens. The Court ordinarily insists upon oral argument, even if the parties are willing to dispense with it.[51]

Ordinarily two cases a day are scheduled for hearing, with one hour being allowed to each side in each case. Variations are possible in either direction, however.[52] If the Justices, in agreeing to review a case on the merits, are of the opinion that less time is necessary, they schedule it for summary argument, in which event each side will be allowed only one half hour. This has been happening with increasing frequency in recent years. If, on the other hand, the case is an exceptionally difficult one, the Court, on application of counsel made in advance, may grant as much additional time as it considers necessary. Thus, in the pending controversy between California and other western states over rights to the waters of the Colorado River, it heard 16 hours of argument in early 1962 and then, the case not having been decided by the end of the term, scheduled an additional 6 hours of reargument for the fall. This case, however, is probably unique in the modern history of the Court, involving as it does, many states with separate interests. Arguments in excess of two hours are allowed very rarely indeed.

The normal pattern of argument is as follows: the appellant opens; then the appellee speaks; then the appellant, if he desires to say anything by way of rebuttal, speaks again. At any stage, the Justices may and usually do interject questions. The time consumed in answering them counts against the time allotted counsel, although occasionally the Chief Justice extends the time if the questioning has been extensive. Even when this happens, however, counsel may be interrupted by further questioning during the extended time allowed him.

No time ordinarily is consumed in reading materials aloud. In fact, so strongly do the Justices feel on this subject that they have virtually prohibited the practice by an explicit Court rule: "The Court looks with disfavor on any oral argument that is read from a prepared text." [53]

Some of the Justices make it a practice to read the briefs prior to hearing oral argument; some do not. All of them, however, have some advance knowledge of each case from having studied the preliminary application for review and from having participated in the conference where the Court decided to hear the merits. Furthermore, because of their specialized function discussed earlier, they are likely to know a great deal about the governing law—the relevant cases, statutes, and constitutional provisions.

At the time of hearing argument, no Justice knows whether he will write an opinion in the case. That will be decided at a future conference.

Each argument is recorded through microphones, one at counsels' lectern and one in front of each of the Justices. No transcription is made, but the tape is available to be replayed in chambers by any Justice who wishes to hear the argument again. This often proves helpful in the drafting of opinions.

The Conference

A conference of all the Justices is held on Friday of each week of argument and on every other Friday preceding a Monday on which opinions are to be announced. It starts at 10:30 A.M. and continues until the business at hand is disposed of—usually five or six hours. The conference is conducted in such strict secrecy that the junior Associate Justice must act as messenger whenever there is a knock on the door.

In addition to applications for plenary review, already discussed, there are two other items on the agenda. The first consists of the cases just heard, usually six or eight during the week. Each is discussed to the extent necessary for the Court to reach a tentative decision. This may take a few minutes or more than an hour. Discussion proceeds, by established tradition, from the Chief Justice to the senior Associate Justice, to the next senior, and so on down to the junior member of the Court. Voting proceeds in the reverse order: starting with the junior Associate Justice and ending with the Chief Justice. Since the conference takes place so shortly after the cases have been heard, it is fair to assume that voting ordinarily must be based upon what the Justices recall from the oral arguments and preliminary study.

At the end of two weeks of argument (in other words, not every week), the writing of opinions is assigned. If the Chief Justice voted with the majority, he designates who shall write the opinion of the Court; but if he voted with the minority, the senior Associate Justice in the majority assigns the writing of the Court's opinion. It is understood by all concerned that the assignments and the votes on which they are based are tentative. Any Justice is free to change his mind at any time before the decision of the Court is publicly announced.

The third item of business on the agenda of the conference is the consideration of opinions in cases already considered and voted upon. Ordinarily, however, this takes little time. The reason is that all opinions—majority, dissenting, and concurring—have been circulated in advance and each Justice has decided upon his position. All that needs to be done at the conference, therefore, is record the final result.

Opinions

The Justice to whom the drafting of a majority opinion has been assigned faces a difficult task. First, he must study the briefs and the record on appeal and conduct such independent research as he deems necessary. Second, he must produce a document which, if it does not convince all of his colleagues or at least those who voted with him during the conference, will at the very minimum command the assent of a bare majority of the Justices. If it fails to do so, it will not be the opinion of the Court. For this reason, numerous informal discussions and interchanges of memoranda with particular Justices may be necessary, accompanied, perhaps, by a succession of redrafts of the proposed opinion.

Once the opinion is in such shape as to satisfy its draftsman (who may or may not by this time have conferred with some of his colleagues), it is circulated to the other members of the Court. If any one of them disagrees with the result or the reasoning—as the result either of earlier consideration of the case or of mature reflection after seeing the proposed opinion for the Court—he decides whether he will prepare a separate opinion. Theoretically, it is possible for the Court to produce nine opinions in a single case, but this extreme is never reached in fact. Very often, however, clusters of agreement are developed and separately expressed in majority, dissenting, and concurring opinions.

Each Justice preparing a minority opinion goes through substantially the same process as the Justice preparing the majority opinion, seeking to obtain agreement from as many of his colleagues as possible, and circulating his draft to all. When all proposed opinions have been circulated and informally discussed to the extent desired, each Justice reaches his own final conclusion, which may or may not be in accordance with his vote at the time of the original conference on the case.

Unanimous opinions are reached in only about 25 percent of the cases considered on the merits by the Court.[54] These, however, usually include those occasional cases which can hardly be described except as earth-shaking in their importance.[55] In the remaining cases, dissenting or concurring opinions are filed, sometimes both. During the course of a year, each Justice writes, on the average, 13 majority opinions and nine dissenting or concurring opinions.[56]

Some persons deplore the lack of a united voice for the Court. The late Charles Evans Hughes, Associate and later Chief Justice, stated this position and then gave his answer to it in these words:

When unanimity can be obtained without sacrifice of conviction, it strongly commends the decision to public confidence. But unanimity which is merely formal, which is recorded at the expense of strong, conflicting views, is not desirable in a court of last resort, whatever may be the effect upon public opinion at the time. This is so because what must ultimately sustain the court in public confidence is the character and independence of the judges. They are not there simply to decide cases, but to decide them as they think they should be decided, and while it may be regrettable that they cannot always agree, it is better that their independence should be maintained and recognized than that unanimity should be secured through its sacrifice. . . .

Dissenting opinions enable a judge to express his individuality. He is not under the compulsion of speaking for the court and thus of securing the concurrence of a majority. In dissenting, he is a free lance. A dissent in a court of last resort is an appeal to the brooding spirit of the law, to the intelligence of a future day, when a later decision may possibly correct the error into which the dissenting judge believes the court to have been betrayed.[57]

In view of the substantial volume of opinions produced by the Court, some observers [58] have been puzzled by their generally high quality. Many of them are so extensively researched and carefully reasoned that they are small treatises of high quality. Many are so well expressed that they have earned a place in general literature.[59]

One partial explanation, it is believed, lies in the fact already mentioned: that the Court is a specialized tribunal, highly expert in the field of its special concern—constitutional law. Another partial explanation must lie in the great amount of time that the Justices devote to their labors. It is quite obvious that they do not adhere to anything like a 40-hour week, and that many do not take much personal advantage of their long summer recess. It is true that the Court does not rise for the summer until all cases ready for decision have been disposed of, but this is misleading. If the Justices feel that a case in which they have heard argument presents exceptional difficulty, they set it down for reargument the following fall. This allows them to continue working on it during the summer.[60] Furthermore, applications for review continue to come in during the summer. While the cases so presented have not been fully briefed, there is nothing to prevent the Justices from studying intensively those which they consider worthy of full review. Their own not inconsiderable resources in the form of specialized background knowledge and assistance from highly competent law clerks are sufficient to allow them to proceed reasonably well even without the assistance of counsel.

Some persons, however, both within the Court and outside of it, demand a still higher standard of performance. Their chief spokesman, perhaps, is Mr. Justice Frankfurter, who says:

. . . the judgments of this Court are collective judgments. Such judgments presuppose ample time and freshness of mind for private study and reflection in preparation for discussion at Conference. Without adequate study there cannot be adequate reflection; without adequate reflection there cannot be adequate discussion; without adequate discussion there cannot be that fruitful interchange of minds which is indispensable to thoughtful, unhurried decision and its formulation in learned and impressive opinions. It is therefore imperative that the docket of the Court be kept down so that its volume does not preclude wise adjudication. This can be avoided only if the Court rigorously excludes any case from coming here that does not rise to the significance of inescapability in meeting the responsibilities vested in this Court.[61]

The crucial issue, in his view as well as in the view of most other responsible critics,[62] lies in the initial selection of cases for review—a matter already discussed. If too many cases are accepted for review or if they are of the wrong type, the work of the Court inevitably will suffer.

In response, Mr. Justice Douglas has stated:

. . . we have fewer oral arguments than we once had, fewer opinions to write, and shorter weeks to work. I do not recall any time in my twenty years or more of service on the Court when we had more time for research, deliberation, debate, and meditation.[63]

When all opinions in a case are in final form, with the positions of all Justices duly noted, they are read aloud or summarized in open court in a ceremony that takes places almost every Monday. This occurs, on the average, about two months after oral argument. Thereafter, the opinions are printed in slip form and distributed to federal and state supreme court judges throughout the nation as well as to selected libraries and law schools. Finally they appear in both the advance sheets and bound volumes of three sets of books: (1) the official "United States Reports"; (2) the "Supreme Court Reporter," published by West Publishing Company; and (3) the "Lawyer's Edition," published by the Lawyers Cooperative Publishing Company.

Finality

The announcement of the Court's decision is not quite the end of the road for the disappointed litigant. He may still apply for a rehearing. In view of the fact that no further appeal is possible, this right is a vital one.

It is exercised by filing a printed petition (40 copies, as usual) with the Court. The petition is considered in the same manner as are petitions for certiorari, except that no brief in opposition is allowed unless and until requested by the Court. If the Court is disposed to grant the petition, a brief in opposition is asked, submitted, and considered before the Court makes a definitive ruling.[64] Most petitions are denied. In the 1960 term, not a single one was granted.

The attitude of the Justices toward such petitions was well expressed by Mr. Justice Bradley from the bench:

It ought to be understood, or at least believed, whether it is true or not, that this Court, being a Court of last resort, gives great consideration to cases of importance and involving consequences like this, and there should be a finality somewhere. This custom of making motions for a rehearing is not a custom to be encouraged. It prevails in some States as a matter of ordinary practice to grant a rehearing on a mere application for it, but that practice we do not consider a legitimate one in this Court. It is possible that in the haste of examining cases before us, we sometimes overlook something, and then we are willing to have that pointed out, but to consider that this Court will re-examine the matter and change its judgment on a case, it seems to me, is not taking a proper view of the function of this Court. Your application is a proper one to be made, but this matter of motions for rehearing has become—I won't say a nuisance, but very disagreeable to the Court.[65]

Nevertheless, some petitions are successful. Thus in 1956, the Court, three Justices dissenting, upheld the constitutionality of the trial of wives of servicemen by court-martial. In the following year, after a rehearing, the Court, again by a divided vote, withdrew its previous decision and held that such trial was unconstitutional. There is at least one case on record where, after one unsuccessful petition for rehearing, a second was submitted and granted (reluctantly). The Court then unanimously reversed its former decision.[66] Today the Court has a rule explicitly prohibiting successive petitions for rehearing.[67]

In a broader sense, however, decisions are always subject to reconsideration—not in the cases in which they were rendered to be sure, but in future cases raising similar problems. The Court is unwilling to be permanently bound by its own prior decisions. The American public is equally unwilling to accept any answer as final, even when given by the Supreme Court, as is evidenced by the spectacle of continuing litigation over racial integration in the public schools five years after a unanimous decision by the

Court.[68] These two circumstances combine to produce a situation in which dissenting opinions are sometimes metamorphosed by the passage of time into prevailing doctrine. Thus in 1938 in the case of Erie Railroad v. Tompkins,[69] the Court embraced views which had been expressed in a dissent by Mr. Justice Holmes in 1928,[70] overruling in the process a decision which had stood since 1842 [71] and all of its numerous progeny. In 1961, in Mapp v. Ohio,[72] the Court adopted a position which it had rejected in Wolf v. Colorado,[73] decided in 1949, and the concurring opinions in the new case quoted with approval the views that had been expressed in the dissents in the old case. Similar examples could be multiplied.

II

ENGLISH APPEALS

CHAPTER SIX

Civil Cases

THE COURT OF APPEAL *

General Description and Place in Judicial Hierarchy

For most civil cases, the Court of Appeal is both the first and the final appellate court for England and Wales.[1] Above it is the House of Lords, but very few cases go that far, and below it are the Divisional Courts of the High Court, but their civil jurisdiction is relatively narrow.

The Court of Appeal hears virtually no criminal cases.[2] They normally go to its counterpart, the Court of Criminal Appeal.

Cases reach the Court of Appeal either from the county courts or from the civil side of the High Court. These require brief description here.

The county courts are manned by some 80 judges, and organized into circuits covering all of England and Wales.[3] Their jurisdiction is exclusively civil, but quite broad, excluding in general only matrimonial cases, defamation cases, and cases involving a substantial amount of money (over £400 in law actions, £500 in equity matters).[4] Most of the proceedings are to collect small claims and are uncontested.[5] Of the relatively few that are contested, trial is almost always by the judge alone, the jury hav-

* © 1962 Yale Law Journal Company, Inc. Much of the information upon which this paper is based was furnished by the Master of the Rolls, Lord Evershed, and Lord Justice Diplock of the Court of Appeal, to both of whom the writer is deeply indebted. Needless to say, they bear no responsibility for the opinions or value judgments expressed herein. Thanks are also due to Mr. R. P. Colinvaux and Miss J. F. Lamb, editor and assistant editor, respectively, of the *Law Reports,* and Mr. C. Lacey Fisher, assistant librarian of the Bar Library, for their help in understanding the English doctrine of precedent.

ing virtually disappeared in the county court.[6] There are no shorthand reporters, with the consequence that records on appeal must
be based upon the judge's longhand notes. As his judgment is usually given orally at the conclusion of the oral argument, there are
no judge's notes of this and it is usual for counsel to make their
own longhand notes and, in the event of appeal, to agree on a draft
which is submitted to the judge for his approval. On questions of
law, appeal lies as of right to the Court of Appeal if the claim
exceeds £20 or the remedy sought is an injunction. Otherwise
leave must be granted by the county court judge. On questions
of fact, appeal lies as of right when the amount in controversy
exceeds £200.[7]

The High Court handles all civil cases which are beyond the
jurisdiction of the county court, as well as some which are within
that jurisdiction. If a case is brought in the High Court which
could have been brought in county court, it may be transferred
there or allowed to continue under the threat that the plaintiff's
costs, if he is successful, will be only such as he would have re-
covered if his action had proceeded in county court.

The High Court is divided into three divisions: the Queen's
Bench Division, consisting of the Lord Chief Justice and 34 puisne
judges, and handling important criminal cases as well as contract,
tort, and other common-law cases; the Chancery Division, consisting of seven puisne judges,[8] and handling what formerly were
known as equity matters; and the Probate, Divorce, and Admiralty Division, consisting of a President and 11 puisne judges,
and handling those matters indicated by its title.

The Chancery Division sits only in London. Judges of the
Queen's Bench Division, while sitting normally in London, also
hold court elsewhere "on assize," hearing important civil and
criminal cases.[9] The manpower of the Probate, Divorce, and Admiralty Division, which sits both in London and a limited number of assize towns, is reinforced by commissioners, including
county judges, who hear divorce cases (defended as well as unde-
fended) in London and in 42 "divorce towns" throughout the
United Kingdom.[10]

As in the county court, very few civil cases in the High Court are heard by jury.[11] All cases are appealable as of right both as to law and fact to the Court of Appeal.[12] The record on appeal consists in large part of a verbatim transcript of proceedings below taken by shorthand.[13]

Place and Time of Sitting

The Court of Appeal sits only in London. Because of the size of England and Wales, because transport to London is good, and because the legal profession is heavily concentrated in that city, this does not seem to cause undue inconvenience.

The court sits in four divisions of three judges each, with each division hearing appeals five days each week during term times. The personnel of the individual divisions is changed from time to time. There are four terms a year: Michaelmas, starting at the beginning of October and running until shortly before Christmas; Hilary, starting in the second week in January and running until the Thursday before Easter; Easter, starting about one week after Easter and running six weeks until the Friday before Whitsunday; and Trinity, starting a week after Whitsun and running until the end of July. In addition to the three short vacations between terms, there is a long vacation of two months' duration in August and September.

Each division convenes daily at 10:30 in the morning and runs to 1 P.M., and then again at 2 in the afternoon, running until 4:15 P.M. Until very recently it was the practice of the court, if a case concluded at 11:30 in the morning or 3:30 in the afternoon, to proceed immediately to the hearing of another. Now the custom is developing in such circumstances for the court to rise, reserving its decision until the beginning of the next regularly scheduled session. This allows the judges time to confer and to draft carefully the critical parts of the judgment (or judgments) to be rendered. The new practice is made possible by the recent enlargement of the court from three divisions to four.

The times for holding court have a significant influence on the way in which appeals are handled. They are well adapted to the English practice of concentrating upon one case at a time and ordinarily rendering a decision immediately upon the close of argument. They would be ill adapted to the American practice of hearing several appeals at a time and customarily reserving decision. Little time in chambers is provided for the English judges to study papers or to write opinions. Hence, when a decision is reserved, the judges are usually forced to work on it evenings or weekends.

Personnel

In practice, the Court of Appeal is composed of the Master of the Rolls and 11 Lords Justices of Appeal, sitting in four divisions of three judges each. The Lord Chancellor has power to assign High Court judges to assist temporarily when circumstances require additional manpower, but in view of the recent enlargement of the court (from nine judges sitting in three divisions to 12 judges sitting in four divisions), this should not be necessary except in case of absence for illness. The Lord Chancellor also has power to assign Lords Justices of Appeal to act as High Court judges in the trial of cases at first instance.

The administrative head of the court is the Master of the Rolls, who determines the composition of each division and the cases which are sent to it. It is customary to send common-law cases to a division composed of two judges who, while at the bar, practiced in that branch of the law and another whose training was in a different branch; to send equity cases to a division having a majority of judges trained in equity, and so forth. Fresh assignments of judges to divisions are made at the beginning of each term.

The Master of the Rolls presides in the division in which he sits and ordinarily delivers the first and "leading" opinion in each case heard by it. In each of the other divisions, the senior Lord Justice assigned to it presides. It lies within the discretion of the presiding Lord Justice to invite other members of the division to deliver the leading opinions in particular cases, and some of them often do so.

The judges hold office for life during good behavior, but are subject by a recent law to retirement on pension at age 75.[14] This age limit applies only to members of the bench who were first appointed in 1960 or after. Politics seems to play no role in their selection today. To be appointed, a man must be a barrister of at least 15 years' standing or an existing High Court judge.[15] Most Lords Justices on the Court of Appeal have previously served as trial judges on the High Court. All of the present members have done so. They are appointed by the Crown on the recommendation of the Prime Minister who is, however, guided by the Lord Chancellor. Salaries (£8,000 for Lords Justices and £9,000 for the Master of the Rolls) [16] are sufficient to attract leading members of the bar.

Unlike their brothers who sit on the Court of Criminal Appeal, the Lords Justices of Appeal are engaged exclusively in appellate work. They do not try cases in the first instance save exceptionally when asked to do so by the Lord Chancellor. They never sit in judgment on the work of their immediate colleagues. The judges do not have law clerks, nor are they provided with any other form of research assistance.

Counsel who appear before the court are trained advocates. As barristers, they are not only specialists in litigation, but also usually specialists in the particular type of case they are arguing. They have gained experience first by "deviling" for older advocates in their chambers (drafting pleadings, preparing memoranda of law, and the like) and then by handling cases on their own. They are selected not by uninformed lay clients, but by solicitors who are also trained lawyers and who make it an important part of their business to know which barristers are best fitted to handle which types of cases. The decision to prosecute or defend an appeal by a particular advocate is an intensely pragmatic process. The specter of heavy costs being assessed against the unsuccessful party induces caution. A solicitor is not likely to retain a barrister who is incompetent, for fear of losing not only the case, but also the client; and the barrister himself is not likely to undertake a hopeless case for fear of losing his reputation, and with it his livelihood. This ensures a level of competency in advocacy which would be hard, if not impossible, to duplicate in a system where the legal profession was not separated into two branches and where costs were not a serious discouragement to frivolous litigation. The court itself is a principal beneficiary, for it is spared having to hear cases which are hardly worthy of consideration, and it almost always receives genuine, rather than token, assistance from counsel.

Volume of Work

In recent years, about 700 appeals a year have been filed in the Court of Appeal. About 150 to 200 are usually withdrawn before argument, leaving 400 to 600 [17] to be dealt with on the merits. These figures show a slight tendency to increase with the recent increases in the number of High Court judges of first instance. Since the court now sits in four divisions, each consisting of three judges, the caseload per division can be expected to average 100 to 150 cases per year. Each case takes, on the average, about a day and a quarter of the time of the division concerned.

Most appeals come from the High Court—373 out of a total of 582 in 1959 and 482 out of a total of 718 in 1960. The bulk of the remainder come from the county courts—187 in 1959 and 193 in 1960.

The volume of appeals is small in relation to the volume of trial litigation. Out of 21,577 trials in the county courts in 1959 (1,325,798 cases were initiated), 187 appeals were taken, but 68 were withdrawn, leaving only 119 to be heard. This is about one-half of one percent of the cases tried. The ratio of appeals to trials in the High Court is higher, but not as high as might be expected. The Queen's Bench Division produces far more appeals than any other division, but only about seven percent of the cases tried by it reach the Court of Appeal.

The relatively small number of appeals is probably explained in part by the expense involved, and particularly by the rule that the loser pays all costs incurred by the other side, including reasonable attorney's fees. In part it is probably due to the fact that a high proportion of actions in the Queen's Bench Division are negligence actions for personal injuries which turn solely upon questions of fact and which therefore are unlikely to be successfully appealed.

Nevertheless, the Court of Appeal reviews determinations of fact as well as determinations of law.[18] It is often said that the appeal is a rehearing. This does not mean that evidence is taken anew, but merely that the scope of review is virtually as broad as the scope of the original trial. In reviewing cases tried without juries (as almost all civil cases in England are), the court refuses to interfere with a trial determination that is based upon credibility. It accords full recognition to the superior position of the trial judge to decide such questions because of his opportunity to see and hear the witnesses. Where his decision turns not upon credibility but upon inference, however, the judges of the Court of Appeal feel less inhibited. Since the drawing of inferences depends upon general information and experience and upon logic, they feel that their collective judgment may properly be substituted for that of the individual judgment of the trial judge, although they will not revise his inferences of fact unless they feel that they are clearly erroneous.

Precedent

In dealing with questions of law, the court follows a doctrine of precedent which seems rigid to American eyes. It considers itself bound not only by decisions of the House of Lords, but also by its own, refusing to overrule them even if convinced that they are outmoded or mistaken. On the other hand, it frequently distinguishes them, sometimes to the point of virtually confining them to their particular facts, and it has available to it various avenues of escape from unwanted precedents. One is the conception that a decision rendered per incuriam, meaning in circumstances where the court was unaware of a controlling line of authority, is not binding. Another is the idea that the court is free to choose not only between conflicting precedents, but also between divergent opinions in the same case. English decisions seldom take the form of opinions by the court, with agreed (or at least majority-approved) texts. Each judge customarily delivers his own opinion, with the consequence that there may be three or five statements from which the court at a later date may choose a *ratio decedendi* for the case at hand.

Even more significant than judicial techniques in handling precedent is the fact that the court is dealing with a body of case law that is remarkably flexible and manageable. That is because there is so little of it. Not all decisions are published—far from it. Only about 25 percent of those rendered by the Court of Appeal appear in the officially sanctioned (though not officially published) *Weekly Law Reports*. About 70 percent of those rendered by the House of Lords and the Privy Council appear, and about 10 percent of those rendered by the Court of Criminal Appeal. The main body of case law from all the courts of England, including not only those mentioned but other appellate and trial courts as well, grows at the rate of only three volumes a year. This is the standard output of both the *Weekly Law Reports* and the competitive *All-England Reports* (which contain in general identically the same cases).

Even so, about a third of the decisions so published are widely considered to be of only temporary interest, for the *Law Reports* proper (printed later, intended to be bound, more carefully edited, and, most important of all, supplemented by rather fuller résumés of the arguments of counsel) do not reproduce them. Some law offices throw away their advance sheets of the *Weekly Law Reports* as soon as the advance sheets of the regular *Law Reports,* published monthly, appear.

The volume of English case law presents a striking contrast to that found in the United States, where the Supreme Court alone produces annually three volumes of roughly equivalent size to those yielded by all the English courts combined. The state courts of New York, serving a population approximately one-third of that in England and Wales, produce about a dozen such volumes each year. These do not include the several additional volumes yielded annually by the lower federal courts sitting in the state.

The cases published in England are chosen not by the judges but by barristers who report them in a manner to be described in detail later in this chapter. The basis upon which they exercise their discretion is precedent value. If a decision announces a principle of law, they deem it worthy of publication, but if it merely applies a well-settled principle to a particular state of facts, they do not. The distinction is easy to state, but hard to apply in view of the recurring but divergent fact patterns that constantly arise. Nevertheless it is applied by trained barrister-reporters, acting under experienced editorial leadership and in the light of long-established traditions. It is heartily supported by most lawyers and judges, not a few of whom would like to see the number of published decisions reduced even further. They like to see the law remain simple and compact, consisting of a relatively small number of broadly stated principles rather than a wilderness of single instances. They also like the saving of cost, not only in terms of the money spent on lawbooks, but also and more importantly in terms of the saving of time of lawyers and judges in preparing and deciding cases.

Nevertheless, there are counterforces working in the direction of fuller reporting. Rules of law almost inevitably evolve from recurring patterns. If facts A, B, and C yield a certain legal consequence as to Mr. Smith—if, for example, they are held to constitute "negligence" in a personal injury case or "extreme cruelty" in a divorce case, or if they are held to justify a certain quantum of damages or a certain type and degree of criminal punishment— it is not unreasonable to expect that they will bring about the same result with respect to Mr. Jones. Otherwise, equality before the law would tend to disappear.

This is probably why specialized reports, supplementing the regular reports already discussed, flourish in England. One series deals with patent cases, another with local government cases, another with traffic cases, several with tax cases, and so on. Each series carries not only the cases in the regular reports within its field of interest but also some (though still by no means all) additional cases within that field. Such reports are partly the result of and partly the cause of specialization within the legal profession. As already indicated, a barrister is typically not only a specialist in litigation, but also a specialist in a certain type of litigation. If he handles commercial cases, he ordinarily has nothing to do with matrimonial cases or will contests. Hence his office (for he is usually in chambers with several other barristers specializing in the same field) subscribes only to the specialized reports that deal with his specialty. He is thus able to keep abreast of decisions on diverse but recurring fact patterns which fall within the broad sweep of the general principles appearing in the cases published in the standard law reports. And since he argues to judges who are also specialists (for example, a division of the Court of Appeal hearing chancery cases includes two judges who were trained at the bar in such cases), there is little likelihood that the court will be unaware of how earlier cases based upon fact patterns similar to the one at hand were decided. Such cases may never be cited by counsel in argument, or by the judges in their opinions, but the memory of them is important and influential upon decision nevertheless. In this sense, the common law of England is far more truly "unwritten" than the common law of the United States.

The consequence is that English judges enjoy a broad discretion in molding the law to fit changing circumstances—broader perhaps than that of judges in the United States, with their power to overrule earlier decisions. In England, with less voluminous reports, there are fewer precedents to cause trouble or to restrict judicial freedom of action.

One final factor affecting the English doctrine of precedent requires comment. That is the machinery for securing legislative corrections of the law. In 1934, the Lord Chancellor established a standing committee, composed of judges, barristers, solicitors, and professors, to study and report on needed changes in the law. Known as the Law Revision Committee, it functioned until the outbreak of World War II in 1939. In 1952 it was reconstituted as the Law Reform Committee and has been supplemented from time to time by ad hoc committees specially appointed by the government to deal with particular problems. Considering suggestions emanating from any source within the legal profession (though formally referred to it by the Lord Chancellor), operating through specially appointed subcommittees of experts, and having access to the wellsprings of legislative power through a secretariat in the Lord Chancellor's Office,[19] this committee has been responsible for fundamental changes in the law. Representative of its accomplishments is the abolition of the doctrine of contributory negligence in favor of comparative negligence and the substantial elimination of the statute of frauds—accomplishments which American courts, despite their relaxed attitude toward precedent, could hardly have been expected to undertake. Certainly on major problems the Law Reform Committee has functioned well. But with minor problems it has not concerned itself, possibly because they are not the special responsibility of any individual group or agency. On such problems, corrective action seems to be taken more easily by the American practice of judges overruling decisions than by the English practice of waiting for legislation.

Statutory Interpretation

The existence of the Law Reform Committee also helps to explain the English approach to statutory interpretation. It tends to be more literal than the American approach, stressing the language of a statute more than its purpose. In particular, the Court of Appeal, in common with other English courts, refuses to consult committee reports or parliamentary debates as aids to ascertaining legislative intention.

The judges are likely already to know something about the background of any statute they are called upon to construe. Perhaps their knowledge comes from random conversations in the Inns of Court where they lunch almost daily with practicing barristers, some of them members of Parliament. Perhaps one of the judges may have participated, as a member of the Law Reform Committee or otherwise, in the deliberations which led to its enactment. In any event, few if any of the judges seem to feel a need for extrinsic aids of the type used in the United States.

Furthermore, the judges assume that, if they make a mistake in ascertaining legislative intent, means are at hand to correct it. Just as the Law Reform Committee and similar governmental bodies outside of the courts can propose legislation to deal with defects in judge-made law, so also they can propose amendments to existing statutes. The unitary nature of the British Government, wherein the Lord Chancellor serves not only as the highest judge of the nation, but also as a powerful legislator and a key member of the Cabinet, lends a weight to recommendations of committees appointed by him which would not be accorded to similar recommendations of bodies similarly constituted in the United States. Nevertheless, it is an open question whether legislative changes, especially on seemingly minor points which are of interest only to a few individuals affected by them, come quickly or easily enough. Responsible opinion in England seems to think that the answer lies in a less literal approach to statutory language, in allowing the judges freedom to reason by analogy from statutory principles, and in less detailed legislative draftsmanship.[20] Deliberately, it does not envisage the use of extrinsic aids to interpretation.

Mechanics of Appeal Before the Hearing

An appeal is initiated by serving on the respondent a notice of appeal within six weeks after entry of the formal judgment in the trial court.

This document specifies the grounds of appeal and the precise relief sought.[21] Since briefs (in the American sense) are not used in England, a delimitation of the area of argument can be accomplished only by some writing filed at an early stage of the appeal. The notice of appeal permits the record to be abbreviated in such a way as to eliminate matter irrelevant to the questions to be considered. The document is an important one, binding upon counsel unless the court (upon motion, almost invariably postponed to the actual hearing of the appeal), allows the assignment of errors to be amended.[22] For this reason, it is usually prepared with the advice of the barrister who handled the trial if he is going to argue the appeal. If not, it is normally prepared by the solicitor for the appellant. Because of its limiting effect it tends to be couched in wide terms which fail to concentrate attention in advance upon the precise points to be argued.

Within seven days of the service of this document on the respondent, it must be filed in duplicate along with a copy of the judgment, and the respondent notified of that fact within two days.[23] If the respondent desires to support the judgment upon some ground other than was relied upon by the judge below, or if he desires to have the judgment varied on appeal, he must serve and file a notice to that effect within 21 days.[24]

The next step is for the appellant to file what in the United States would be called a record on appeal, consisting of the formal papers in the case (notice of appeal, judgment, pleadings, and list of exhibits), plus excerpts from the stenographic transcript of the proceedings below.[25] These include the opinion of the trial judge and whatever testimony and exhibits are relevant to the questions raised on appeal.[26]

It is customary in England for the trial judge to deliver a reasoned opinion, citing authorities, rather than to rely, as in most trial courts of the United States, upon formalized "findings of fact and conclusions of law" or upon the judge's instructions to the jury. This tends to formulate the issues that will be discussed upon appeal as well as to inform the appellate court quickly of the nature of the case.

As for the exhibits and testimony, if unnecessary material is reproduced, the appellant receives no reimbursement for the cost thereof, even if he succeeds upon the appeal. This is regarded as a serious sanction in England, and is enforced by taxing masters.[27]

Seldom is there any dispute between English lawyers as to what ought to be included in the record on appeal. If the respondent (appellee) desires to add to the record and cannot obtain the agreement of the appellant, he is entitled to do so at the risk of paying the costs thereof, even if he is successful on the appeal, if the court considers the additional matter unnecessary.

The record on appeal is mimeographed, not printed. Only three copies are required, one for each of the judges who will be sitting.

No rigid time is fixed for filing the record on appeal. It is supposed to be done at least one week before the case appears on the daily cause list. This time can be ascertained by inquiring in the clerk's office and by following the published daily cause list. When filed, the papers go to the clerk of the Lord Justice who will preside in the division to which the case has been assigned—a matter which also can be ascertained in advance. The time lapse between the filing of the notice of appeal and the argument averages about six months. This represents a sharp improvement over the situation which prevailed until the recent increase in the size of the court. When there were only three divisions, the average time lapse was about a year.

No other papers are filed beyond those mentioned. In particular, there are no briefs.

Oral Argument

Judges of the Court of Appeal hear cases one at a time and ordinarily without advance preparation. They sit in open court day after day throughout an entire term, hearing arguments and deciding cases. Except between terms and except when the court occasionally rises early (see above), there are no periods of recess in which they may study the appeal papers or prepare the decisions.

Because the English method of arriving at judicial conclusions is based upon the use of oral argument, there are no briefs for them to read, and the judges ordinarily learn all they are to know about a case from the oral arguments of counsel. They have the record on appeal before them shortly before the oral hearing, and those who so desire can read it. This record includes the reasoned opinion of the court below, which summarizes the facts and discusses the questions of law, citing all the authorities that the trial judge regarded as relevant. If they do not take this course (and many prefer not to do so), and so see the record for the first time at the actual hearing, they must, in order to use it for any purpose other than note-taking, master the art of reading and listening at the same time.

Counsel do not content themselves with telling the judges briefly and in narrative form what the case is about and what questions are raised upon appeal. They read extensively from the testimony, the documents, and the judgment below, interpolating comments as they go. This occurs whether or not there is any dispute as to what happened in the court below. The reading takes approximately half of the entire time devoted to an appeal.

Besides reading the judgment and the evidence below, counsel also read aloud from the legal authorities, statutory or otherwise, to which they wish to call the court's attention. When this is done, the judges are furnished with copies of the books involved so that they may follow with their eyes what they are hearing from the lips of counsel. An advantage of dealing with legal authorities in this way is that counsel cite relatively few of them, not a dozen when one would be enough. Sometimes counsel do not cite even a single case. When the governing legal principles are well settled, it may be safely assumed that the judges know and will apply them.

Reading often tends to be either too fast or too slow. It is likely to be too fast when the complicated language of a statute or lease is involved. It is likely to be too slow when testimony is involved. There is, moreover, a danger of distortion in reading testimony aloud, because, through emphasis and pace, the words of a witness uttered conversationally may be analyzed and dissected as though they were the product of deliberate draftsmanship.

Questioning by the judges tends to be fairly extensive. They feel no inhibition in discussing with counsel who is addressing them the case before them and the authorities claimed to govern its decision, or in revealing the trend of their thoughts as the case progresses. They rely upon this kind of Socratic process in open court to clarify the issues of fact and law. Questions or comments addressed to counsel may well be directed to persuading their fellow justices, thus fulfilling to a degree the purpose of post-hearing conferences between the judges in American practice. They thus become involved immediately, consciously and deliberately, in attempting to reach a decision while the oral argument is in process. In truth, an appeal sometimes has the appearance of a committee meeting with five members present, only three of whom have a vote.

Sometimes after argument has been in progress for a while, the presiding judge tells counsel for the appellant that the court "need not trouble" him further. This is an indication that the judges have reached a tentative conclusion in his favor either on the whole case or on specified points. They are ready, in other words, to hear the other side. The burden of going forward with the argument is thus shifted to counsel for the respondent. It is up to him to persuade the judges that their tentative conclusion is wrong.

In much the same way, the argument of counsel for the respondent may be curtailed. The court may announce that it wishes to hear argument only on a certain point, thus indicating that the judges have decided against the appellant on all other points. Or it may dispense with argument from the respondent entirely. If, after hearing counsel for the appellant, the judges have reached the conclusion that the decision should be affirmed, they see no point in spending time hearing the respondent. The presiding judge merely announces that the court wishes to hear no further argument and then proceeds to deliver his opinion.

Except for such informal, ad hoc controls as have just been described, the time for argument is unlimited. The average case takes about a day and a quarter to hear, but some cases run into weeks while others take only an hour or so.

An Experiment to Curtail Reading

Shortly after the Anglo-American interchange described in Chapter 1, the Court of Appeal conducted an experiment aimed at cutting down the amount of time consumed in open-court reading. Lord Evershed, then Master of the Rolls, announced it in open court on March 22, 1962. His remarks were reported in *The Times* of the next day as follows:

The Master of the Rolls, presiding in the Court of Appeal, announced that, in view of comments by United States jurists on our appellate system, immediate steps would be taken by way only of experiment with the aim of reducing the time taken in the hearing of appeals by the Court. In particular documents would be read by members of the Court before the hearing of an appeal.

Referring to the visit last July of a distinguished party of American lawyers led by Mr. Justice Brennan, his Lordship said that its object was to examine and compare the work in our two countries of appellate courts, civil and criminal. A return visit was paid to the United States in January of this year by a similar English team (of which Lord Evershed had been the leader).

TIME OF READING

"Following these visits," continued his Lordship, "the members of each team have recorded their comments upon the appellate system in the country of the other team. The comments of the American team about our own system have been both generous and gratifying; but all the American visitors, without exception, have drawn attention to the length of time so frequently taken in this Court by the reading of documents, including the judgment under appeal and the cases therein cited; and it has been pointed out (with truth) that the result must often be substantially to increase the costs which, under our system, one or other of the parties or (in appropriate cases) in whole or part the Legal Aid Fund will have to pay.

"The point is indeed the same point that was taken in the Final Report of the Committee on Supreme Court Practice and Procedure which therefore recommended (a) that an appellant should in his notice of appeal be bound to state the grounds of his appeal and (b) that the appeal judges should, before hearing a case, have read the notice of appeal and the judgment appealed from—or the relevant part of it.

HOMEWORK FOR JUDGES

"It has not been suggested by any member of the English team that we should in this country adopt the American system of 'written briefs' and the limitation of time spent on oral arguments. On the other hand the unanimity of the American comments, which added to the recommendations of the Committee on Supreme Court Practice, have persuaded my colleagues and myself in this Court that it would be worth while making an experiment aimed at a real reduction in the time taken, through mere recitation, in this Court and therefore at a real reduction in costs; but without at all fettering the right of counsel to full oral argument of their cases. For the purposes of such experiment each member of the Court will have read (1) the pleadings or the originating summons (or their equivalent) (2) the order under appeal (3) the notice of appeal and respondent's notice (if any) and (4) the judgment of the learned judge, together with any cases cited by him in his judgment. It is proposed to introduce the experiment in this Court with the Appeals Tribunal List next week and so in each such appeal we shall all have read beforehand the case stated, the order made by the Tribunal, the notice of appeal and the decision, together with any cases cited in the decision.

"In order that the judges shall have time and opportunity to read what is mentioned above, the Court may on occasion sit at a somewhat later hour; but due notice will be given of this."

What was suggested, his Lordship emphasised, was by way of experiment; the results would depend on the event. It was only by trying that you could learn. He was sure that all would agree that the experiment should be tried, and hoped that counsel and solicitors concerned would co-operate with the Court in the attempt. The proposal was made with the full support of the Lord Chancellor, and representatives of the Bar and the Law Society had been consulted.

At the beginning of the Easter term (about May 1st), the experiment was extended to all four divisions of the Court of Appeal. Then, at the end of the term, all of its judges met to appraise the results. They concluded that advance reading of the papers on appeal and precedents worked well in some cases, not well in others; and that the practice should henceforth be reserved for "long, heavy" appeals.

Such is the practice today, and it is no longer regarded as experimental. The presiding judge of each division of the court, assisted by his clerk, scans the papers in each case a few days before it is due to be reached for argument. If he finds that the appeal is likely to be short and simple (the great majority of appeals are of this type), he lets the case take its normal course described earlier. If, on the other hand, he concludes that the appeal is likely to be so long and complex as to warrant reading the papers beforehand, he notifies his brother judges to that effect. Then they have three or four days before the hearing in which to do their "homework." At the same time, counsel who are to appear in the case are notified, so that they may prepare their presentations in the light of the fact that the judges will have already read the papers.

Sometimes in the middle of an appeal, the judges decide that it would be well to read some of the papers overnight, and they proceed to do so. Thus, in a recent appeal involving about a hundred pages of correspondence, the presiding judge announced to counsel on both sides that the judges would read that correspondence by the time the court convened the next morning at 10:30 A.M. That procedure was followed, and a considerable amount of time saved. This happens fairly often.

The Decision

Customarily, though not invariably, the court renders its decision immediately upon the close of argument. Each judge speaks, no one of them with any greater authority than either of his colleagues. The senior judge, who is also presiding judge, delivers his opinion first, extemporaneously. It is sometimes described as the "leading" opinion. Then the other two judges state, also extemporaneously but somewhat more briefly, their opinions. Often the second and third judges, especially the latter, will say little more than that they concur with the views already expressed. Sometimes one of them develops an alternative ground of decision or registers a dissent. Dissents are relatively rare, occurring in a small percentage of cases; but so also are single opinions for the court as a whole. All opinions are recorded in shorthand and later transcribed.

In the ordinary case, there has been little opportunity for collective deliberation between the judges. They always have a whispered conversation, seldom lasting more than a minute or two, on the bench, or a brief talk in the corridor while walking to or from the courtroom, but they are not likely to attempt anything further in the way of a conference. And since opinions are not written, but delivered extemporaneously, there is only limited opportunity for an advance interchange of suggestions and comments.

Nor are the judges individually able to carry on any profound independent study of a case or to spend much time in meditating, deliberating, and reflecting after hearing the oral argument. That is because ordinarily no interval elapses between the conclusion of argument and the rendition of the decision.

What has just been described above is the ordinary case where the judgment is delivered immediately upon the close of oral argument. It is becoming increasingly common, however, for judges to postpone decision overnight or over a weekend. When this happens, the situation is somewhat altered. There is still little time for study, reflection, or discussion or for writing out opinions at length; but there is some. The major part of any opinion still probably will have to be delivered extemporaneously when the court convenes, but the interval is generally taken and used for reducing to writing the crucial part of the opinion.

Less frequently, decision may be reserved for as long as a week or a month. This provides an opportunity for study, reflection, and discussion if the judges can find time during evenings and weekends. They cannot find it during the regular working days, for those must be devoted to hearing and deciding other appeals, save in the rare case where they take a day or half a day's recess for this purpose. For this and other reasons, the judges are reluctant to reserve decision. They prefer to deal with one case at a time and to dispose of it finally before turning to another.

Once the decision is announced, nothing remains to be done except to pass upon a possible motion by the disappointed litigant for leave to appeal to the House of Lords. Such a motion is made orally and immediately and is decided summarily. If denied, the moving party can apply for leave to the House of Lords itself.

Rearguments in the Court of Appeal are unknown.

Law Reporting and Publishing

The opinions are taken down verbatim by shorthand writers. When transcribed, they are submitted to the judges who rendered them for possible revision. Some judges take advantage of the opportunity to do a careful editing job, particularly if they think that the case is one which is likely to be published in the *Law Re-*

ports. Others do not, preferring to rely on the law reporters for whatever editing is needed.

One copy of each set of opinions is then filed in the Bar Library in the Royal Courts of Justice, a library open, except upon special permission, only to judges, barristers, and their clerks. They are indexed according to name, date, the court from which the appeal came, the judges who participated, and subject matter.

Whether ultimately published or not, these opinions can be cited as precedents, and they are to a limited extent, particularly if they deal with such questions as the quantum of damages in personal-injury cases or if they are so recent as not to have had a chance to find their way into the published reports. Several factors, however, militate against any very extensive use of them. First, they are not readily accessible. Only one copy is available in the whole of England. Ordinarily the only cases the librarians are asked for are those whose existence is already known to the researcher—perhaps not by name or exact date but by some type of lead. Except by writers of textbooks (some of whom cite these opinions extensively) they are not systematically studied. Second and more important, the judges tend to discourage the citation of unpublished opinions. Imbued with the philosophy of law reporting described above, they regard relatively few decisions as having precedent value, and are inclined to pay little attention to factual comparisons between the case at bar and earlier cases. They are disposed to accept the judgment of those who edit the *Law Reports* that the only cases worth citing are those which appear in the published volumes.

Nevertheless, the unpublished decisions are lying around like unexploded land mines, ready to do damage. For the lawyer industrious enough to search them out or to keep track of those he encounters, they may prove to be highly useful. Their existence may also help to explain the doctrine mentioned earlier whereby the Court of Appeal may avoid following a precedent on the ground that it was rendered per incuriam—that is, in ignorance of some controlling prior decision.

About one-fourth of the decisions of the court are published in the *Weekly Law Reports*. This series, which has been described above in general terms, is the basic repository for modern English cases, forming the basis for the so-called "permanent" *Law Reports* proper. While it is supplemented by various specialized reports as well as by a competitive series of general reports (the *All-England* series), the way in which it is prepared will give a fair indication of how law reports generally come into existence.

The *Weekly Law Reports* are published by the Incorporated Council of Law Reporting for England and Wales, a quasi-official, nonprofit organization composed of a judge as chairman, the Attorney General, the Solicitor General, and representatives of the four Inns of Court, the Law Society (the central organization for solicitors), and the General Council of the Bar (the central organization for barristers). Members of the Council meet three or four times a year and concern themselves primarily with the business aspects of the enterprise—how much staff members should be paid, where funds of the Council should be invested, and the like. They undoubtedly possess power to determine editorial policy as to what cases or kinds of cases should be published and in what manner, but in practice they leave the choice of individual cases to the staff.

The staff consists of an editor, an assistant editor, about 25 full-time reporters, and about 10 part-time reporters. All are barristers, some women and some men. They occupy a vital role in determining the shape of English law. Their job is to cover all the courts of record of England and to report whatever decisions are worthy of preservation. The criteria they use have already been described.

The principal appellate courts of the nation, namely the House of Lords, the Privy Council, the Court of Appeal, and the Court of Criminal Appeal, are covered systematically, with a reporter in virtually full-time attendance at every sitting. Other courts, trial or appellate, are covered only to the extent that the editors and reporters anticipate interesting or important happenings. Since the reporters contribute to *The Times* (newspaper reporting of legal subjects in England is remarkably full and accurate) and to specialist journals of the type already described as well as to the *Weekly Law Reports,* and since they are constantly on the alert to learn about significant cases from their acquaintances among the judges, barristers, and solicitors, they are not likely to miss many cases of real importance. Nevertheless, because of the impossibility of covering all courts at all times with a staff so limited, the only trial-court decisions likely to be reported are those rare ones in which the judge recognizes the matter to be of such importance that he takes the trouble to write out his opinion in full instead of delivering it orally, as is the usual custom.

The decision to report a case lies in the first instance with the reporter responsible for the court in which it was decided. If he is inexperienced or if for any other reason he fails to appreciate the significance of a case, there is a possibility that it will be lost forever as a precedent. It can be cited if a transcript of the judgment can be found in the Bar Library (though only decisions of the Court of Appeal and the House of Lords are available there) or if it is reported by any barrister; but as a practical matter it has to be found first. Any oversights by the reporters, however, are likely to be corrected by the editors, who frequently have their attention called by judges, barristers, and solicitors to cases that ought to be reported. Apart from acting upon such suggestions, the main function of the editors with respect to determining the cases to be published is to exercise veto power on cases which they feel do not belong in the *Reports*. Despite their care and despite the strong sense of responsibility exercised by the reporters, mistakes occasionally happen and have to be rectified (as when frequent calls by the bench and bar for an unreported decision lead to its publication in the *Reports* a year or two later). Nevertheless, in general the system works well in carrying out the English ideal of reporting all cases which announce principles of law, but only those—omitting ones which simply turn upon their own particular facts. This is attested by the fact that the Council of Law Reporting, representing the entire legal profession, has never, since its establishment in 1865, found it necessary to interfere with the details of editorial policy. Whatever dangers may exist in the present system are thought by the English legal profession generally to be less than those which would inhere in a system of reporting all cases, including many which only applied well-settled principles to specific fact patterns. Under such a system, with its multiplication of volumes of printed material, it is feared that vital cases might be overlooked in the masses of unimportant cases reported.

Once a decision has been made to report a given case, heavy work for the reporter lies ahead. His task is not merely to collect and transmit to the printer a document which is ready for publication but to do an editorial job of great delicacy and importance. The first thing he does is to order from the shorthand writer a transcript of the decision after it has been seen (and perhaps revised) by the judges. Then he sets to work. He verifies all names, dates, and places mentioned; he checks all citations to statutes, cases, and other authorities; he restates the facts clearly and concisely; and he rewords the judges' opinions in such a way as to preserve their meaning but improve their style, by eliminating redundancy and polishing grammar. His object is clarification without alteration of substance. If the case is one destined to be published in the *Law Reports* proper (as distinguished from the *Weekly Law Reports*), the reporter also prepares a summary of the arguments of counsel on both sides, with an indication of any significant comments and questions interposed by the judges. In doing all of this work, the reporter is aided not only by whatever notes he has made while listening to the case, but also by a borrowed copy of the record and by access to the notes, papers, and recollections of counsel.

Most barristers are happy to cooperate, realizing, as they do, that this is one of the few avenues by which their names and work may become known. Finally the reporter prepares appropriate headnotes.

After a report has been put into such form that the reporter and editors believe it is ready for publication, it is printed in galley form and submitted for final correction to the judges and barristers involved. Sometimes there are penciled queries and suggestions in the margin. After these have been answered and the report approved (usually without further corrections) it is published.

The net result of the editorial process just described is that published reports sometimes bear little resemblance to the judgments, delivered orally and extemporaneously, upon which they are based. What sounds in court like a long, rambling discourse, with incomplete sentences and doubtful syntax, may turn out in print to be a polished composition, just as if the judge himself had taken the time and trouble to write it out in full.

With written judgments such as are customarily rendered by the House of Lords and Privy Council and occasionally by the Court of Appeal, the reporters take fewer liberties. They do not alter language except to correct obvious errors in names, places, citations, etc. They do, however, excise portions of the opinions which they consider unilluminating, indicating the omissions by brackets. The theory is that omissions are not alterations. They also tend to deal rather freely with the facts, choosing the one statement—out of perhaps three or five in the separate opinions—which seems most apt, and sometimes even redrafting that one. Then they indicate what they have done by saying "the following statement of facts is based on the judgment of Mudd, LJ," or words to that effect.

The law reporter in England performs many of the same functions as are performed by the law clerk in the United States. He does not participate in the process of formulating a decision in the first instance (but then neither do some American law clerks, depending on the judges for whom they work), but he renders the same kinds of service after that point has been reached. His responsibility however, is not so clearly fixed, for he is not directly answerable to any judge or group of judges. While in one sense his influence is less than that of the typical law clerk, in another sense his power is greater. Having a considerable measure of control over what cases are to be published and in what form, he determines to a very large extent the content of the English case law for the future.

CHAPTER SEVEN

Criminal Cases

THE COURT OF CRIMINAL APPEAL *

General Description and Place in Judicial Hierarchy

For all except one or two cases a year which go as far as the House of Lords, the Court of Criminal Appeal is the final criminal appellate court for England and Wales. It has no concern with civil cases.

Appeals reach it either from "assizes" or from quarter-sessions courts.[1] Assizes are held in various towns throughout England and Wales for the hearing of very serious criminal cases, such as murder and armed robbery.[2] They are almost always presided over by judges from the Queen's Bench Division traveling on circuit. The assize in London is held in the Central Criminal Court, better known as "Old Bailey." Almost all trials are by jury.

Quarter-sessions courts (originally so called because they met four times a year) are empowered to try most but not all serious crimes, lacking power, for example, to handle cases carrying the death penalty or those in which life imprisonment can be imposed for a first conviction.[3] They are organized on a county basis, and each court is composed of all magistrates in a given county, although not more than nine of its members sit at any one session. A jury is almost always present. Its function is to determine guilt or innocence, whereas the court itself is primarily concerned

---

* © 1962 American Bar Association. Much of the information herein was furnished by the Lord Chief Justice of England, Lord Parker of Waddington, and Lord Justice Diplock of the Court of Appeal, formerly Judge of the Queen's Bench Division of the High Court, to both of whom the writer is deeply indebted. They bear no responsibility for the opinions or value judgments expressed herein.

with sentencing. The presiding magistrate (in all counties today he is a lawyer and very often he is a judge of high rank serving on a volunteer basis in his spare time) rules on questions of evidence and procedure during the course of the trial and instructs the jury. Most of the larger cities and towns have their own quarter sessions, consisting of a single part-time judge known as a "Recorder" who is always a senior barrister, frequently a Queen's Counsel. He is a paid official, unlike the presiding magistrates for the quarter-sessions courts in the rural counties. All rural magistrates are unpaid, but they take their work very seriously indeed, and they enjoy a very high measure of prestige.

Personnel

The Court of Criminal Appeal has no judges of its own. Its members are drawn from the Queen's Bench Division of the High Court. This is true even of the head of the court, the Lord Chief Justice. He also administers the Queen's Bench Division, and sits in it as a trial judge when time permits. Most of his time, however, is occupied in administration and in presiding over the Court of Criminal Appeal and the Divisional Court. The latter is another appellate tribunal within the Queen's Bench Division which hears appeals in criminal cases tried by magistrates and reviews, by means of the prerogative writs, the actions of administrative agencies and local government bodies.

Thus the judges who hear criminal appeals devote less than full time to that task. Most of the energies of the judges who sit with the Lord Chief Justice are devoted to trial work; while in London they are engaged mainly in trying civil cases, and while traveling on the assize circuit they are engaged more than half their time in trying criminal cases.[4] They sit in the Court of Criminal Appeal only when designated for such service by the Lord Chief Justice, just as they might be assigned by him to any other type of service within the Queen's Bench Division. So far as possible, assignments are rotated often enough to allow each judge to hear criminal appeals at least once each term [5] that he is sitting in London (not on assize).

The court does not sit en banc, but in panels. The usual number of judges is three, but it can be increased at the discretion of the Lord Chief Justice for especially important or difficult cases to five, seven, or conceivably the full membership of the Queen's Bench Division.

One consequence of the judges serving both at the trial and appellate levels is that they sit in judgment on the work of their immediate colleagues. One term Judge A may be sitting on the Court of Criminal Appeal reviewing a case tried by Judge B on assize. The next term Judge B may be sitting on the court reviewing a case tried by Judge A on assize.

Another consequence is that each judge quickly receives a well-rounded education in accustomed judicial ways. This is especially important for the newly appointed judge, who may have had little or no experience in criminal cases. What he learns while sitting on the Court of Criminal Appeal helps him when he is trying cases on assize (and very likely also when he is trying civil cases). What he learns at the trial level illuminates the problems he faces when hearing appeals. There is no gulf of misunderstanding between appellate and trial judges, such as sometimes develops in systems where the judges who hear appeals do no trial work.

Stability in criminal-law enforcement would seem to be an almost inevitable by-product of the English system. The judges, staying closely in touch with each other and keeping abreast of the changing picture of crime throughout the country, are enabled to maintain a high degree of uniformity in their sentences.

The only regular member of the Court of Criminal Appeal is the Lord Chief Justice. He ordinarily participates in the hearing of all appeals except those few in which he was involved below as trial judge. When he sits, he invariably presides and generally delivers the first, and almost always the only, opinion.

To be eligible for appointment as a Queen's Bench judge, a person must be a barrister of at least ten years' standing; for appointment to the post of Lord Chief Justice, he must already be a High Court judge or a barrister of at least fifteen years' standing. The Lord Chief Justice is appointed by the Crown on the advice of the Prime Minister after he has consulted with the Lord Chancellor. The other judges are appointed by the Crown on the advice of the Lord Chancellor alone. All of the offices carry tenure during good behavior until retirement on pension at age 75 (although there is no compulsory retirement age for those appointed before 1960). The salary of a Queen's Bench judge is £8,000 per year; that of the Lord Chief Justice is £10,000. Not only in terms of salary, but also in terms of prestige and power (he is a peer, and thus anomalously but in common with other highly placed members of the English judiciary, a legislator as well as a judge, and he is a member ex officio of the other principal appellate courts as well as head of the Court of Criminal Appeal, the Divisional Court, and the Queen's Bench Division), the Lord Chief Justice is the second highest ranking judicial officer of the realm, standing next to the Lord Chancellor.[6]

The barristers who appear before the court are specialists in litigation, able to communicate effectively and economically with the judges. They are not necessarily highly specialized in criminal law but their expertise generally lies in that field. There are no professional prosecutors (what in the United States are called district attorneys) in England, nor are there any professional "public defenders." A man who appears for the Crown one day may appear for the defense the next.

Not infrequently the barrister will receive his compensation under the legal aid system, which in England is highly developed and quite different from that found in the United States. It makes legal aid (meaning publicly financed legal service) available to indigent prisoners at the appellate level as well as at the trial level. While the service is publicly financed, with the need for it being judicially determined and with fees being judicially fixed, it is rendered by barristers engaged in private practice. There are no legal aid attorneys such as are found in the United States, employed by legal aid societies or the government. Any solicitor or barrister who wishes to take legal aid cases places his name on lists kept for that purpose by the courts, and thus becomes eligible for assignment to the defense of particular cases. Many of the leading advocates of the nation are thus available to represent indigent persons accused of crimes. There is no shortage of willing hands.

Time and Place of Sitting

The court sits in London exclusively.

Until recently it was the custom to have only one panel operating at a time and that only one day a week—Monday. Now there are usually two panels sitting on Monday, and sometimes, if the caseload warrants, on another day as well. The hours are the same as in the Court of Appeal: from 10:30 A.M. to 1 P.M. and from 2 P.M. to 4:15 P.M. unless the day's business is completed sooner.

The Right and Scope of Appeal

The jurisdiction of the court is largely discretionary. The only cases which reach it as a matter of right are those involving a pure question of law, as for example the interpretation of a statute, the correctness of an instruction to a jury, or the legality of a sentence.[7]

For all other appeals, leave to appeal is required. If a conviction is challenged—on the ground, for example, that the evidence is not sufficient to support it—permission can be granted either by the trial court or the Court of Criminal Appeal.[8] If a sentence is challenged on the ground that it is excessive, permission can be granted only by the Court of Criminal Appeal.[9]

Review of convictions (appeals are allowed only by the defendant, never by the government) extends to questions of fact as well as to questions of law. The court, however, is extremely reluctant to interfere with determinations of fact, since in all cases they have been made by juries. While the right to trial by jury is not constitutionally protected in England, it is highly prized nevertheless. Consequently, the Court of Criminal Appeal is more circumscribed in its review of factual determination than its sister tribunal, the Court of Appeal (which deals for the most part with cases tried before judges alone). Provided that the charge to the jury contains no misdirection as to law or fact, and

The Court of Criminal Appeal · *109*

provided there is sufficient evidence to support the verdict rendered, the Court of Criminal Appeal will not interefere with a judgment of conviction.

In dealing with questions of law, the Court of Criminal Appeal also follows a somewhat different approach. It feels less rigidly bound by precedent than the Court of Appeal, and more free to overrule its own prior decisions when convinced that they are mistaken or outmoded. Realizing that it is dealing with the liberty of the people, that appeals to the House of Lords are exceedingly rare, and that parliamentary changes in the law are only prospective in operation, it occasionally departs from the strict doctrine of stare decisis when it feels that such a course is necessary to prevent injustice in a particular case.[10] Even so, overrulings are rarely necessary. A major reason is that there are relatively few precedents to cause difficulty. In general, the only decisions published are those which enunciate principles of law. Those which turn upon their particular facts are not reported.

The court is not empowered to grant a new trial, presumably because of the fear that another trial would violate the principle against double jeopardy, and possibly also because of the idea that trial judges and lawyers should be kept under pressure to do their work correctly the first time, with no hope of a second chance. Hence, if the court finds that an error was committed below, it has to choose between setting the accused free or affirming his conviction on the ground that error did not result in a substantial miscarriage of justice.[11] It cannot follow a middle course of ordering another trial which would be free of the error which infected the first trial. The result is that some guilty persons are turned loose without punishment for no other reason than that errors were committed in their trials. Whether others are punished who might have been acquitted if their trials had been free of error is a question on which there can be no confident answer. Ideally, the answer would be "no," for only harmless errors are supposed to be disregarded by the court when it affirms a conviction. The governing principle is that the court will affirm only if it is convinced, after reviewing all the evidence or acting with the concurrence of counsel for the prisoner, that the jury would have come to the same conclusion if the error had not occurred.

Review of sentences is not confined to the question of their legality; it extends as well to their propriety. If leave to appeal against a sentence is granted, the court may either increase or decrease the sentence.[12] Increases, however, are rare, none having been imposed between 1957 and 1961,[13] in which latter year two or three were increased. Changes in sentence are decreed on a quasi-objective standard—not on the ground that the judges hearing the appeal would have given a different sentence, but on the ground that no judge, in view of the nature of the crime committed and the character of the accused, could reasonably have imposed the sentence in question. If a single judge on the court is strongly in favor of a reduction, it is given. Sentences vary from time to time as the judges estimate the need for deterrence in a particular area or with respect to a particular kind of crime.

Applications for Leave to Appeal

Convicted prisoners are formally notified of their right to seek appellate review by means of printed cards posted in their jail cells. These cards, supplementing whatever informal advice may be given by trial counsel or offered informally by other prisoners and jail officials, provide detailed explanations of legal rights and the procedure to be followed in invoking them.

Most applications for leave to appeal are prepared by the prisoners themselves (on official forms furnished by the jail authorities). That is because in most cases they have been advised by counsel not to appeal. As might be expected, the reasons given in support of the self-drafted applications are not impressive, running to such statements as "I was not guilty" or "My wife is going to have a baby soon." The task of screening worthy applications from unworthy ones therefore falls heavily upon the judges and other officials of the Court of Criminal Appeal.

An application (usually handwritten) goes first to the registrar of the court. He and his legally trained assistants (all are barristers) prepare a record of proceedings below for consideration by the judges. In capital cases, a full transcript of the evidence is always included. In other cases, only the accusation, the transcript of character evidence, and, if the prisoner pleaded not guilty, the charge of the judge below are normally included in the papers initially prepared for judicial scrutiny. The registrar may add some or all of the evidence, but usually does not do so. The judge's charge, in accordance with English practice and in contradistinction to prevailing American practice, summarizes the evidence, thus providing the appellate court with an overall view of the case and the issues presented. It serves the same purpose in a case tried by jury as is served by a reasoned trial judgment in a case tried by a judge alone. Hence the Court of Criminal Appeal is furnished with roughly the same kind of help from the trial bench as is given to the Court of Appeal in civil cases.

These papers, including the application for leave to appeal, are then sent to one of the judges assigned to the Court of Criminal Appeal. He may, before reaching a decision, demand all or part of the transcript of evidence. If he decides to grant leave, the case is scheduled for hearing before the court. If he decides against it, that fact is communicated to the prisoner, who may then drop any further attempt to secure review. In 1960, out of 2,279 applications for leave to appeal, 859 were denied by a single judge and then abandoned.

If a prisoner, upon being notified of the denial of his application by a single judge, insists upon it, his application will be considered by a full panel of the Court of Criminal Appeal.[14] When this happens, the time that elapses between resubmission of the application and the decision thereon does not count as part of the prisoner's sentence—a fact which may account in part for the abandoning of many attempts at appellate review after an adverse decision by a single judge. Even more significant may be the fear of the prisoner (whether well or ill founded) that his sentence may be increased if he persists. The granting by the court *sua sponte* of legal aid to the prisoner for the prosecution of an appeal on sentence tends to be regarded as a signal that the court may be considering an increase in the sentence.

If the entire court is asked to consider the application, each judge on the panel receives a set of the papers already described, together with a brief memorandum summarizing the case prepared by the registrar or one of his assistants. One of the three judges, however, is assigned primary responsibility for announcing the decisions of the court for each case on a rotational basis. That is, Judge A gets case No. 1, Judge B case No. 2, Judge C case No. 3, Judge A case No. 4, and so forth. The judges individually consider all of the applications (usually over a weekend preceding the Monday on which court will be sitting) and then meet for a very brief conference immediately before their sitting. If any one of them is in favor of granting leave to appeal (not necessarily the judge to whom the case was assigned), leave is granted. Sometimes the judges demand a transcript of all or part of the evidence as a preliminary to reaching their conclusion.

In the year 1960, the court denied 1,145 applications for leave to appeal. Adding these to the number denied by a single judge (859), we see that only 275 appeals were heard on the merits. This is about 10 percent of the applications and about 1 percent of the convictions in the courts below. In the cases heard, only 42 convictions were quashed, but 127 sentences were reduced. The remaining cases were affirmed. The percentage of successful applications is very small indeed—something like 6 percent of the applications dealing with sentence and 4 percent of those dealing with conviction.

Papers on Appeal

The same papers that are used on an application for leave to appeal are used on the appeal itself, supplemented, if the judges so desire, by part or all of the transcript of evidence. As in the Court of Appeal, so also in the Court of Criminal Appeal: no written arguments or briefs are submitted.

Oral Argument

All the judges study the record before starting the oral hearing. Thus, unlike the judges of the Court of Appeal, they never approach a case cold. They are spared having to listen to counsel read the record at length. The only reading that is likely to take place is from legal authorities cited by counsel—an almost inescapable procedure since there are no briefs and the decision is rendered immediately upon the close of oral argument.

Seldom are more than two or three cases cited to the court, frequently none. Counsel ordinarily may take for granted that the judges are familiar with the governing legal principles—an assumption justified not only by the specialization of the court, but also by the small bulk of reported cases. Unnecessary citations are explicitly discouraged by the judges.

The consequence of dispensing with as much reading as possible is that oral argument tends to be relatively short in duration, averaging not more than about 20 or 30 minutes per case. More lengthy arguments occasionally take place, but they are exceptional. It is not uncommon for the court to dispense with oral argument by the respondent. If the judges are satisfied after hearing counsel for the appellant that the judgment should be affirmed, they see no point in wasting time listening to the other side.

Ordinarily, the prisoner whose appeal is being heard is present in court. He has that right unless the appeal is concerned exclusively with a point of law, in which case the prisoner's presence is discretionary with the court.

Newly Discovered Evidence

An unusual feature of the court's procedure concerns its power to hear evidence.[15] This power is used only a few times a year and only if the evidence offered was not available to counsel for the prisoner (acting with due diligence) at the time of trial. When the Court of Criminal Appeal hears such evidence, it not only holds the line against retrials in criminal cases, but also saves the time which in the United States would have to be consumed in rehearing the case in its entirety. On the other hand, it is confronted with the difficult and delicate task of deciding what effect the new evidence would have had on the jury if it had been able to hear it.

The Decision

In the Court of Criminal Appeal, even more than in the Court of Appeal, the practice of rendering decision immediately upon the close of oral argument is followed. Very rarely indeed is decision reserved. Hence there is little time for discussion between the judges (except in the form of brief talks in advance of argument or whispered conversations at the bench) and no time for the drafting of opinions. Judgments are delivered extemporaneously except in the rare case where the court merely announces its decision and reserves until a later day the statement of its reasons.

In contrast to the practice prevailing in the Court of Appeal, the judge who is presiding almost invariably delivers the only opinion in the case. The other judges remain silent unless (as very rarely happens) the court makes an explicit finding that the case involves a question of law of substantial importance. If upon a quick conference of the judges on the bench it should appear that one of them was likely to dissent, the case would be rescheduled for argument before a larger panel, consisting of five, seven, or more judges. This scarcely ever happens. A statistical comparison of the number of opinions delivered by the Lord Chief Justice with the number delivered by all other members of the court reveals that he tends to be the chief, almost the exclusive, spokesman for the court in appeals (as distinguished from applications for leave to appeal).

Expedition of Decision

Most criminal appeals are heard and decided promptly. The only time that ordinarily elapses between the imposition of sentence in the trial court and the decision in the appellate court is that which is consumed in the preparation of the necessary papers on appeal. Here the only bottleneck is likely to be the securing of a stenographic transcript of the evidence where that is necessary (see above). Even with that bottleneck, it is a rare case in which more than a month elapses between the sentence and the decision of the appeal. This is as true for capital and other very serious cases as it is for relatively minor cases.

Publication of Opinions

Only about one-tenth of the opinions of the Court of Criminal Appeal are published. This is because the majority of them deal only with the propriety of sentences, and, being factual determinations, are regarded as having little value as precedents. The same principle which governs the reporting of decisions of the Court of Appeal also governs the reporting of those rendered by the Court of Criminal Appeal. Selections are made by the law reporters on the basis of their estimate of the value of the cases as precedents. While unpublished decisions of the Court of Criminal Appeal are not available in the Bar Library, they can, on request, be examined in the office of the court.

Finality of Appeal

Appeal is the only normal, almost exclusive, legal procedure for reviewing a criminal judgment. Collateral attack is not allowed, neither habeas corpus nor coram nobis being available for this purpose.

If something which invalidates the trial is discovered after the normal time to appeal has expired, an application can be made for leave to appeal "out of time." There is no inexorable time limit on the taking of appeals.

Further review in the House of Lords is possible under the circumstances stated in the description of that court, but it is extremely rare.

If an appeal has already been heard at the time when a fact which justifies relief is discovered, application is made to the Home Secretary.[16] That official can refer the case to the Court of Criminal Appeal for its advice, or can handle the matter administratively, deciding for himself (sometimes on the basis of solicited advice from the court or a distinguished barrister, specially appointed) whether there is justification for relief from the judgment or sentence.

CHAPTER EIGHT

Ultimate Review

THE HOUSE OF LORDS

AND THE PRIVY COUNCIL *

General Description and Place in Judicial Hierarchy

The House of Lords is a judicial as well as a legislative body. Being the High Court of Parliament, it is the ultimate tribunal for the United Kingdom, hearing appeals from England and Wales, Scotland and Northern Ireland.[1] In it is vested the ancient jurisdiction of the Queen in Parliament as the supreme court of the realm. The fact that it is a legislative body as well as a judicial tribunal significantly affects its methods of operation.

The Judicial Committee of the Privy Council is the highest tribunal for such of the Commonwealth nations as have chosen to retain the right of appeal to it, including Australia, New Zealand, Ceylon, and Nigeria, as well as many smaller and less highly developed nations.[2] Nevertheless, historically and in theory, the Privy Council is not a "court" in the traditional sense, but a committee of advisers to the sovereign. Its methods of operation reflect that fact.

Within the legal profession, however, these two tribunals are regarded as "courts." It will be convenient in this paper to adopt

---

* Much of the information upon which this paper is based was furnished by Lord Denning, formerly Lord of Appeal in Ordinary, now Master of the Rolls; Sir George Coldstream, permanent secretary to the Lord Chancellor and Clerk of the Crown in Chancery; Mr. R. P. Cave, principal clerk in the Judicial Office, House of Lords; and Mr. A. J. N. Paterson, the registrar of the Judicial Committee of the Privy Council, to all of whom the writer is deeply indebted.

that terminology, inexact though it may be. Furthermore, they are regarded as twin tribunals, manned by the same personnel by and large, and performing the same kind of work. The only substantial difference between them is in the location of the courts from which their appeals come. For this reason, the following description, though phrased mostly in terms of the operations of the House of Lords, is intended to cover the Privy Council as well. Where significant differences exist, they are pointed out.

Jurisdiction

The only cases which reach the House of Lords of the Privy Council have been heard on appeal once before—in the Court of Appeal or the Court of Criminal Appeal or Courts-Martial Appeal Court in England or in their counterparts in other nations.[3] Civil cases go to the House of Lords from England and Wales, Scotland and Northern Ireland; criminal cases only from England and Wales and Northern Ireland, not Scotland. The Privy Council receives both civil and criminal cases from the Commonwealth nations.

While both courts have jurisdiction over criminal appeals, they have thus far heard very few of them. In the year 1959, the House of Lords did not hear a single one; in the year 1960 it heard only two. The average has been one every other year.[4] Until recently, such appeals could be taken only upon the fiat of the Attorney General (or in some circumstances, the Solicitor General) declaring that the case involved a point of law of exceptional public importance. In 1960 the power to determine which appeals should be allowed was vested in the courts; now the Court of Criminal Appeal (or in certain cases, a divisional court of the Queen's Bench Division or the Courts-Martial Appeal Court) must certify that a point of law of general public importance is involved in the decision; and, in addition, either that court or the House of Lords itself must grant leave.[5] Whether this change will have the effect of increasing the case load is too early to tell, but it is probable that it will.

The Privy Council likewise hears few criminal cases, refusing to grant leave to appeal unless a showing is made that the question presented involves the fundamental fairness of procedure below. It refuses to interfere with the normal administration of criminal justice in the Commonwealth countries or to examine alleged errors of the type appropriate for review in a court of criminal appeal. The policy was stated in the case of Re Dillett, 12 App. Cases 459, at 467 (1887) in these words:

Such appeals are of rare occurrence; because the rule has been repeatedly laid down and has been invariably followed, that Her Majesty will not review or interfere with the course of criminal proceedings, unless it is shewn that, by a disregard of the forms of legal process, or by some violation of the principles of natural justice, or otherwise, substantial and grave injustice has been done.

Time and Place of Sitting

The House of Lords and the Privy Council sit only in London, even though the latter hears appeals from courts located as far away as Australia. This may be one of the reasons why some important nations in the Commonwealth, including Canada, have discontinued appeals to the Privy Council.[6] Reasons of national prestige, however, have probably had a more important bearing.

Neither tribunal is housed in the building occupied by the Royal Courts of Justice. The House of Lords operates about two miles away in the regular Parliament buildings and the Privy Council in another government building on Downing Street.

There are no fixed dates for the hearing of appeals. Both courts normally sit during legal terms on four days a week from 10:30 A.M. to 1 P.M. and from 2 P.M. to 4 P.M.

Personnel

Nine Lords of Appeal in Ordinary, or "law lords" as they are commonly called, form the backbone of personnel in both courts. They are life peers and thus qualified to act as legislators as well as judges, but by tradition they do not participate in parliamentary debates in which controversial matters of public policy are in issue. They do, however, participate in the consideration of proposed legislation of a purely legal or administrative character.

Most of the law lords have previously served as judges in the lower courts. A typical professional career might be as follows: distinction at the Bar, followed by appointment to the bench of the High Court, followed by elevation to the Court of Appeal, followed by designation as a Lord of Appeal in Ordinary. Seldom is this pattern, or something close to it, broken.

In addition to the law lords, peers who hold or have held high judicial office are qualified to sit.[7] The extent to which they participate depends largely upon their other responsibilities. Thus the present Lord Chief Justice of England is qualified to sit, but rarely does, whereas his predecessor, now retired, sits fairly frequently. Similarly, the Master of the Rolls is qualified to sit, but the ordinary work attached to his office is so heavy that he is rarely called upon. In the Judicial Committee of the Privy Council, certain persons who hold or have held high judicial office and certain judges overseas are also qualified to sit.[8]

At the head of both the House of Lords and the Privy Council is the Lord Chancellor. He is not only a member of the Cabinet and the Speaker of the House of Lords, but also the highest judicial officer of the realm.[9] As administrative head of the entire system in England and Wales, he is responsible not only for judicial appointments, but also for the efficient operation of the courts. As a judge, he can (but in practice does not) sit in the High Court and the Court of Appeal. He presides as often as he can in the House of Lords and the Privy Council, but his appearances are comparatively infrequent because of the press of his other responsibilities. His administrative duties in connection with those courts, however, are extensive. He determines when cases are to be heard and by whom. In other words, he chooses the judges who will hear particular cases. The quorum is three, but the Lord Chancellor can designate a larger number. The usual number is five for the House of Lords, and either three or five for the Privy Council, depending upon the nation from which the appeal comes. Law lords are not assigned to regular panels, but chosen ad hoc for each case by the Lord Chancellor.

Cases are usually conducted by two barristers for each of the parties concerned—a Queen's Counsel and a junior barrister. By their oral and written arguments, they provide the judges with the main help they receive. The judges do not have the assistance of law clerks or other research helpers, nor do they have private secretaries. Any stenographic or clerical help they need is provided from a pool.

Volume of Work

The House of Lords hears a relatively small number of cases. In 1960, 38 appeals were decided, and in 1959, 54. The Privy Council has a roughly equivalent caseload. In 1960, 39 appeals were decided, and in 1959, 29.

Adding together the work of the two courts, the caseload is still small, considering the judicial manpower available. In 1960, the total number of appeals heard by both courts was 77; and in 1959 the total number was 83. Since the judges normally sit in panels of five, each can be expected to participate in about 40 appeals per year.

Against these statistics must be balanced the fact that most of the cases heard are lengthy and difficult, with arguments averaging about three days in duration. This is about twice the amount of time consumed, on the average, by cases heard in the Court of Appeal and many times greater than the average in the Court of Criminal Appeal.

Applications for Leave to Appeal

(A) IN THE HOUSE OF LORDS

The relatively small volume of cases in the House of Lords is explained by the fact that an appeal can be taken only by leave of the court below or of the House of Lords itself. A litigant wishing to appeal makes an oral application to the court which decided against him immediately upon its pronouncement of judgment. That court thereupon summarily grants or denies leave. If leave is granted, the case goes up without further ado. If it is denied, the applicant may address a formal written petition to the House of Lords, attempting to show why the case is one which ought to be further reviewed at the highest level. His application will then be heard orally by a panel of three law lords, sitting as the Appeal Committee and chosen ad hoc for that purpose by the Lord Chancellor. Hearings are held at irregular intervals 10 or 15 times a year, and last normally for a half or a full day. At each sitting three to five applications are likely to be heard, with arguments ranging anywhere from 10 minutes to an hour.

Two or three days in advance of each hearing, the law lords receive and study the petitions and supporting papers (judgments below and statutory provisions, if any, relied on). For this reason, no time need be consumed in reading the papers aloud in court. Litigants may, and frequently do, appear in person; or they may be represented by barristers or, surprisingly enough, by solicitors, or even by a lay "friend." If the applicant fails to persuade the judges that he deserves leave to appeal, they may dispense with argument from the respondent and deny the application forthwith. Decisions are announced immediately, but theoretically do not become operative until approved by the House of Lords a few days later—a pure formality.

If, on the other hand, the three judges, after hearing both sides, are convinced that the case presents a problem of law of substantial public importance—if, for example, it involves the interpretation of a new statute, or a conflict of decisions between the various nations of the kingdom—leave will be granted. About 20 percent of the applications, numbering in total some 50 each year, are successful.

Very few cases go up, whether by permission of the House of Lords itself or of the courts below—on the average less than five percent of those decided in the Court of Appeal in England and less than one percent of those decided in the Court of Criminal Appeal in England.

(B) IN THE PRIVY COUNCIL

The number of cases going to the Privy Council has diminished in recent years as various nations in the Commonwealth have withdrawn permission for appeals to it, e.g., India, Pakistan, Ghana. The last Canadian appeal was heard in 1959. However, the number of appeals from the newer independent nations, e.g., Nigeria, is tending to increase. The jurisdiction of the court is, in effect, dependent upon continued consent of nations within the Commonwealth.[10]

Some cases may be appealed as a matter of right—generally speaking, civil actions where the amount in controversy is £500 or more. All others require permission. In civil actions, such permission may be granted by the court below, or, if it refuses, by the Privy Council itself, whereas in criminal cases, only the Privy Council is empowered to grant leave. The number of petitions, civil and criminal, averages about 50 a year, of which about one-third are granted. The remainder of the 30 or 40 cases heard each year are appealed as of right or by permission of the court below.

The procedure followed in dealing with applications is substantially similar to that in the House of Lords, but these two differences may be observed: (1) the right of audience is granted only to barristers and litigants in person, not solicitors; and (2) hearings on leave to appeal are not necessarily scheduled separately, but often take place just prior to the hearing of an appeal on the merits, no special "Appeal Committee" being designated and the work being considered a normal assignment for any panel which happens to be sitting.

Scope and Nature of Review

Although the law lords are legislators as well as judges, sitting in a body which in one capacity has undoubted power to change the law and in another the ultimate power of judicial review, they tend to maintain the same attitude toward precedent as judges in the courts below. By a self-imposed limitation, which has been the subject of prolonged controversy,[11] they make it a practice never to overrule their own prior decisions.

Some of the explanation may lie in the nature of the subject matter with which they deal. For the most part, it is legislation, which, being subject to correction by ordinary parliamentary processes, presents a problem quite different from that which would be presented by a written constitution changeable only by a far more cumbersome procedure.

While many of the precedents by which the court feels bound are the House's interpretations of statutes, some are judge-made in their entirety. These common-law rules owe their existence solely to the law lords themselves or their predecessors, not to the House of Lords as a legislative body or to Parliament as a whole. Nevertheless, the judges feel themselves as much bound by these precedents as by the others.

A curious phenomenon is the relationship between precedents in the House of Lords and those in the Privy Council. Decisions of the latter do not bind the former, and decisions of the former do not bind the latter, although all decisions are made by the same group of judges. Even more curious is the fact that the judges when sitting as Privy Counsellors feel free to reconsider their own previous decisions,[12] but when sitting as members of the House of Lords, feel bound by them.

In the field of statutory interpretation, which occupies much of the attention of both the Privy Council and the House of Lords, another self-limiting doctrine prevails. The law lords decline to make use of legislative history to inform their judgment. They sedulously avoid committee reports, parliamentary debates, and similar extrinsic aids of the kind relied upon so heavily in the United States. Being peers themselves, however, and frequently members of government committees considering law reform, they may have actual personal knowledge of the intention of Parliament in framing a particular piece of legislation.

Preliminaries to Oral Argument

Unlike the courts below, the House of Lords and the Privy Council receive written arguments in advance of hearing, somewhat similar to the briefs used in American appellate courts. These "cases," as they are called, recount the facts, the proceedings below, the contentions of the parties, and the authorities relied on. They do not present arguments at length or go into the detail found in American briefs. They seldom run more than six or eight pages in length, and perhaps can best be described as advance written outlines of oral arguments to be presented later.

Both the case of the appellant and that of the respondent are required to be presented to the opposing side as well as filed in court. In the House of Lords this is supposed to take place within six weeks after the appeal is filed. The appellant may in fact file and serve his case within that time, but he frequently asks and receives an extension of time. On the other hand, the respondent ordinarily does not file and serve his case until about two weeks later. In the Privy Council no rigid time limits are imposed, since much depends on the amount of time required to secure the record on appeal from abroad. In neither the Privy Council nor in the House of Lords is the respondent's case necessarily an answer to that of the appellant. It is an independent argument in support of the judgment below, and in the Privy Council the respondent's case not infrequently is served and filed before that of the appellant.

A few days in advance of argument the cases are presented to the judges who will hear the appeal. Accompanying them and bound with them into a single volume (or occasionally several volumes) is the record on appeal. It is substantially the same record as was earlier presented to the court from which the appeal was taken, except for the fact that it contains, in addition to documents reflecting the proceedings in the trial court, those which show the proceedings on appeal below. Most important, it contains the judgment of the Court of Appeal or other court from which the case comes. These documents need not be printed, but are commonly mimeographed (under official supervision), with the judgment of the court below often taken in its already existing printed Law Report form. Their cost is substantially less than the cost of similar documents in many courts of the United States.

In criminal appeals in the House of Lords, cases are not required, whereas in the Privy Council they are, just as they are in civil appeals in both courts.

Oral Argument

In most cases hearings are conducted in an informal atmosphere. The setting is more that of a committee room than a courtroom. The judges do not wear wigs or robes, but ordinary business suits (not even the traditional black jackets and striped trousers of the legal profession in and around the courts of law). They do not sit on a dais or behind a bench, but in ordinary chairs at ordinary tables arranged in a row. The only note of formality is contributed by counsel, who wear their robes and wigs (full-bottomed in the case of Queen's Counsel), and by the doorkeepers, wearing full-dress suits and around their necks gold chains with pendant medallions. In the Privy Council there are two court ushers who wear full-dress suits but no gold chains.

In a few cases (less than ten percent), appeals are heard in the Chamber of the House itself, where the atmosphere is highly formal.

The judges of the House of Lords have before them at the beginning of argument not only the documents already described, but also a one-page summary prepared by the clerk. It shows the nature of the case, the question presented, the judgments below, the allowance of the appeal, and the names of counsel appearing for the respective parties. No similar document is used in the Privy Council.

Despite the fact that the judges have the benefit of advance briefing as well as time between cases for private study, oral argument follows much the same pattern as in the Court of Appeal. Unlimited time is allowed and it is not unheard of for a hearing to go on for 20 or more days, sometimes consuming more time than was consumed in the original trial. The average is about three days.

Much of the time is devoted to listening to the lawyers read aloud from the record and from authorities claimed to support their respective positions. Not infrequently, also, such authorities are examined by the judges during the course of the hearing, with lawbooks piled on their tables.

Almost always both sides are heard. Since every case has been screened in advance to see that it presents a substantial question of law, and since the practice of the judges is to reserve decision, it is unusual for a case to be disposed of after only the argument of the appellant has been heard.

The Decision

When oral argument in a case has been concluded, the judges do not, as in the lower appellate courts, attempt to reach an immediate decision and deliver it orally. They reserve decision until a later date, except in those rare cases where they announce their decision forthwith but reserve the statement of their reasons until a later date. Sometimes, therefore, a given judge or group of judges will hear two or three cases before rendering opinions in any of them. However, since they ordinarily sit four days a week rather than five, and since they feel no compulsion to hear argument during every hour of each day of sitting (for example, if a case terminates sooner than expected, they may rise rather than go on to a new case), the judges enjoy a modicum of time for work in chambers.

PROCEDURE IN THE HOUSE OF LORDS

In the House of Lords, each judge writes his own opinion and circulates it to the other judges who sat to hear the appeal. They may or may not meet to discuss and attempt to reconcile their views. Formal conferences are rare. It is unusual for an attempt to be made to reach agreement on an "opinion of the court." In the majority of cases each judge is merely preparing to express his individual views.

When all of the judges are ready (usually about six weeks after a case is heard), a special sitting of the House of Lords is called to convene in its regular legislative chamber, and counsel are invited to attend. The Lord Chancellor sits on the Woolsack in full regalia (or in his absence the next senior law lord presides), and prayers are said by a bishop. The chamber is almost empty, however, for the only other persons likely to be in attendance are the judges who heard the appeal and counsel and their instructing solicitors. Counsel, robed and wigged, sit behind a wooden barrier which separates the spectators from the peers. The judges, in their regular business suits, sit on benches in the chamber. No other peers are likely to be present, for those not legally qualified (892 of the 920 members of the House) are permitted only in the capacity of silent spectators. By strong and inflexible tradition, they are not allowed to participate.

Each judge then proceeds to read aloud his opinion save in those unusual cases where a single opinion has been agreed upon for the whole court. One law lord's opinion may differ from those rendered by his colleagues either as to the conclusion to be reached or as to the reasons. Disagreement occurs in about 25 percent of the cases. Despite the fact that all opinions are written out in full and are ready for distribution to the solicitors, counsel, and the press, this procedure consumes a considerable amount of time—sometimes more than two hours. For this reason, one or two of the law lords have recently omitted substantial parts of their opinions rather than reading them in full, but the omitted parts are printed in the *Reports*. When all the judges have spoken, the Lord Chancellor puts the question to the House, and the judges answer "content" or "not content." That concludes the appeal: the judgment below has been affirmed, reversed, or varied.

PROCEDURE IN THE PRIVY COUNCIL

In the Privy Council, the process of reaching a decision diverges sharply from that followed in the House of Lords. Again the reason is found in the special nature of the institution involved.

As the court consists of Privy Counsellors who form a Committee of the Privy Council, the judges are compelled to reach a single opinion, with no dissents or concurrences. That opinion constitutes advice to the Queen, and is invariably followed. Since the Queen cannot act upon the basis of contradictory advice, the judges must conceal whatever differences of opinion they may feel. One of them, designated by the senior judge participating, drafts an opinion and circulates it to his colleagues. All the judges then attempt, by means of discussions, conferences, and redraftings, to reach agreement as to both substance and language. If they are unable to reach agreement, the majority view prevails. Minority points of view remain unexpressed.

The promulgation of the opinion is attended by no such formality as that which prevails in the House of Lords. Its author, or some judge who sat with him on the appeal, simply reads aloud in open court at a regular sitting the last paragraph of the opinion, and then copies of the full opinion are distributed by the clerk to the solicitors, counsel, and the press. No genuine executive approval is required—only pro forma acceptance by the Queen at a formal meeting of the Privy Council. Judicial independence is as absolute in the Judicial Committee of the Privy Council as in any court of the land.

PUBLICATION OF DECISIONS

Despite the fact that appeals to the House of Lords and the Privy Council are allowed only on important questions of law, and despite the small number of decisions rendered, not all of them are published. In 1960, the opinions in only 53 cases were published in the *Weekly Law Reports* out of 77 heard. As in the case of the lower courts, the reporters have the final word as to which decisions are to be published. Unpublished decisions of the House of Lords (not the Privy Council), like those rendered by the Court of Appeal, can be found in the Bar Library.

CHAPTER NINE

Other Appellate Courts in England

THE DIVISIONAL COURTS *

In addition to the courts described in detail in the preceding three chapters, there are other tribunals in England which exercise appellate jurisdiction. Thus the Courts-Martial Appeal Court (which in practice and personnel is almost indistinguishable from the Court of Criminal Appeal) reviews cases tried by courts-martial in the armed forces; and Courts of Quarter Sessions, whose main business is to try serious criminal cases in the first instance, also hear de novo less serious criminal cases appealed from Magistrates' Courts. Similarly, where an appeal lies from a quasi-judicial determination of a governmental body (what in the United States is called an administrative agency), the statute giving the right may provide that the case will be heard by a certain branch or judge of the High Court.

Two tribunals do appellate work of such importance and in such volume that they deserve more than passing reference. These are the Divisional Courts of the Queen's Bench Division and the Probate, Divorce, and Admiralty Division. In terms of direct impact upon the day-to-day affairs of most ordinary citizens, these may well be the most important appellate courts of the nation.

---

* The information upon which this paper is based was furnished in very large part by three judges of the High Court, to whom the writer wishes to express his deep appreciation. They are: Sir Jocelyn Simon, President of the Probate, Divorce, and Admiralty Division; Sir Seymour Karminski, a justice of that division; and Sir Thomas Ashworth, a justice of the Queen's Bench Division. They bear no responsibility, however, for the opinions or value judgments expressed herein.

The Divisional Court of the Queen's Bench Division

This court, frequently referred to simply as the Divisional Court, performs two important functions.

MINOR CRIMINAL CASES

First, it reviews minor criminal cases (motoring offenses, disorderly conduct, petty statutory crimes of all sorts) which have been tried in the first instance by justices of the peace, or, as they are more commonly called, magistrates. These unpaid, highly esteemed officials, who are usually laymen serving in their spare time, handle an immense volume of work, deciding approximately 98 percent of all criminal cases tried in England. A person who has been convicted in a Magistrates' Court can seek review by either of two alternative methods. First, he can have his conviction, his sentence, or both considered de novo on the law or the facts in the Court of Quarter Sessions, a tribunal composed of other magistrates in the county, presided over as a rule by a High Court or county court judge or a barrister of distinction serving in his spare time. (See also Chapter 7.)

Second, he can go to the Divisional Court on a "case stated." This means that a document is prepared for signature by the magistrates which briefly states the charge, the findings on the evidence, the action taken and the reasons therefor (sometimes with the citation of authority), and which then asks in effect whether such action was proper. The document is generally prepared by agreement between the legal representatives of the parties, but, in default of agreement, responsibility for preparing it rests with the magistrates, assisted by their clerk (who generally has legal qualifications). On the basis of this document (which is usually only two or three pages in length), the Divisional Court hears argument and renders its decision.

The procedure just described is useful only if a point of law is involved, for the factual findings and the sentence are not open to review in this manner, but only by means of a trial de novo in Quarter Sessions. Neither is a jurisdictional error or a gross procedural error open to review by means of a case stated. If magistrates act beyond their jurisdiction, or if they have some personal interest in the outcome of a case, the remedy is in the Divisional Court, but by way of one of the prerogative writs (to be described below in connection with the court's control over quasi-judicial administrative action).

The procedure of appealing to the Divisional Court on a case stated is open not only to the convicted defendant, but also to the prosecution if there has been an acquittal. If the Divisional Court reverses, it directs a conviction or acquittal, or remits the case to the magistrates for further consideration in the light of the court's decision.

ADMINISTRATIVE TRIBUNALS

The other major appellate function performed by the Divisional Court concerns governmental agencies other than the traditional courts. Many of these exercise powers of a quasi-judicial nature. With respect to some of them, the acts of Parliament conferring their powers also provide for judicial review of the exercise of those powers in traditional courts—e.g., the Divisional Court, the Court of Appeal, the Court of Chancery, or some other branch of the High Court. With respect to other agencies, no such judicial review is provided. If this is the situation, the Divisional Court moves into the gap, exercising the historic common-law powers represented by the prerogative writs, especially prohibition and certiorari. In theory this is original jurisdiction, but functionally it is appellate, since its object is to reach and correct improper action by another tribunal.

A person who considers himself aggrieved by a quasi-judicial determination of some administrative agency applies to the Divisional Court orally and ex parte for leave to move for an order of certiorari or prohibition. He submits at that time a written statement of the grounds of his action, usually two or three pages in length, supported by affidavits if necessary. The court grants the motion unless it is clearly evident that there is no merit whatever in the application or that the application is out of time.

Then the papers are served on the administrative agency in question and the case comes on for hearing in the usual way. Hardly ever is there any factual dispute, so that the court needs only to deal with the questions of law involved.

The scope of review is limited. The court cannot inquire into the wisdom or lack of wisdom of the action being challenged. It cannot even inquire whether there was sufficient evidence to justify the findings. All it can do is to inquire whether the tribunal exceeded or refused to exercise its jurisdiction, whether it made any error of law apparent on the face of its decision, and whether it conformed to the "principles of natural justice." In practice, this latter ground for review limits the court to deciding if the tribunal allowed a fair hearing, and if it was free of bias or personal interest in the outcome of the proceedings.

Closely related to the court's jurisdiction in prohibition and certiorari is its jurisdiction in habeas corpus. If a person claims to be unjustly imprisoned—not as the result of the judgment of a legal tribunal, but illegally, as for example by virtue of improper extradition proceedings—he may apply for habeas corpus in the Divisional Court. The procedure is virtually the same as described above in connection with prohibition and certiorari.

Because of the historic and continuing significance of the remedy of habeas corpus, because of the importance of control over quasi-judicial administrative action in an age when the scope of governmental action is constantly expanding, and because of the day-to-day impact of reviewing the work of courts which are in close and steady touch with the common run of the citizenry, the Divisional Court plays a role of the utmost importance in the English judicial system.

PERSONNEL AND METHODS OF OPERATION

In personnel, the Divisional Court is closely akin to the Court of Criminal Appeal. The three judges who sit on it are also trial judges of the Queen's Bench, assigned temporarily by the Lord Chief Justice to appellate duties. Very often they are the very same judges who sit in the Court of Criminal Appeal, with the Lord Chief Justice presiding.

The methods of operation of the Divisional Court are also similar to those of the Court of Criminal Appeal. The cases heard by it seldom last more than an hour each (although occasionally one will run for several hours or even several days), and the judges almost always deliver their opinions extemporaneously at the close of argument. The most prominent difference in procedure is that, whereas the presiding judge of the Court of Criminal Appeal delivers the only judgment in the case, each judge of the Divisional Court may express his own views. In this respect, the practice of the Divisional Court more closely resembles that of the Court of Appeal than that of the Court of Criminal Appeal.

The Divisional Court of the Probate, Divorce, and Admiralty Division

Magistrates handle not only the bulk of criminal cases tried in England, but also a very large proportion of the matrimonial cases. Any relief short of divorce in a domestic dispute can be sought in a Magistrates' Court. A very common type is an order of maintenance or separation in favor of a wife against her husband, often coupled with an award of custody of the children to one of the spouses.

In such cases, appeals lie to the Divisional Court of the Probate, Divorce, and Admiralty Division. They are generally heard by the President and one other judge of the division. These men do not devote all of their time to appeals, but most of it to presiding at trials in the first instance. In this respect they operate in a manner not unlike that found in the Queen's Bench Division, whose judges also are engaged primarily in trial work and only occasionally in hearing appeals.

The record on appeal is ordinarily a rather slim document. Since shorthand writers are not available in Magistrates' Courts, there is no verbatim transcript of the testimony, but only notes of the evidence made by the magistrates' clerk. Similarly there is no written judgment, but only a note of the findings and the reasons for them prepared by the clerk and signed by the magistrates. Because of this abbreviated record, the court rarely interferes with factual determinations by the magistrates, although it possesses power to do so in clear cases. It restricts itself rather to reviewing decisions upon issues of law and inferences and value judgments made by the magistrates. Thus the court is often called upon to decide such questions as whether in a particular case the husband's conduct amounts to "cruelty" or whether and to what extent the wife's own earnings and property should be taken into account in determining the allowance for support to her.

Such questions are of great importance not only to the parties directly involved, but also to the law of domestic relations in England generally. This is because, to a very large extent, the same grounds which justify an order in the Magistrates' Court for separate maintenance also justify a divorce in the High Court. Thus a decision on the meaning of adultery or cruelty or condonation in an appeal from a Magistrates' Court to the Divisional Court may become a precedent binding on the judges, the divorce commissioners, and the registrars of the Probate, Divorce, and Admiralty Division of the High Court as they carry on their normal work of handling divorce litigation.

Appellate Procedure in the Divisional Courts

Except in the respects already mentioned, the Divisional Courts of the Queen's Bench and the Probate, Divorce, and Admiralty Divisions conform to the normal English method of handling an appeal. No briefs are used; oral argument is not limited in duration (although it is usually brief since there is little material to be read aloud to the court); and judgments ordinarily are not reserved, but delivered extemporaneously at the conclusion of argument.

As a result partly of the Anglo-American interchange described in Chapter 1, some alterations in procedure have recently been made in the Divisional Court of the Probate, Divorce, and Admiralty Division. The changes are these. First, the judges (ordinarily the President and one other judge of the division) now read the record on appeal in advance of oral argument. Counsel are advised of this fact at the beginning of a case and thus invited (if not virtually required) to desist from reading aloud the judgment and evidence below. Results thus far indicate that the court is able to dispose of its cases in substantially less time than was formerly required. Second, the judges are devoting more time than formerly to the revision of their judgments. They still ordinarily deliver their judgments extemporaneously at the close of oral argument; but now, instead of relying heavily upon the law reporters for editorial assistance in putting the judgments into shape for publication, the judges take over most of that responsibility for themselves. Thus, without sacrificing the peculiar values of their own procedure, they are attempting to capture some of the advantages of the slower, more deliberative American procedure of always rendering reserved, written opinions.

Further appeals from the divisional courts lie as follows: from that of the Probate, Divorce, and Admiralty Division to the Court of Appeal; from that of the Queen's Bench Division to the House of Lords in criminal cases or matters, if leave to appeal is granted, and to the Court of Appeal in noncriminal matters, leave to appeal being required in most cases.

III

COMPARISON

CHAPTER TEN

THE TWO NATIONAL PATTERNS
COMPARED AND CONTRASTED

The American method of handling appeals, though historically derived from England, is today fundamentally different from the English method. In the United States, oral arguments are limited in duration and secondary in importance to written briefs; in England, they are unlimited in duration and of primary importance, written briefs being virtually unknown. In the United States, the judges do most of their work in chambers; in England, they do most of it in open court. In the United States, decisions are ordinarily reserved and handed down in written form; in England, they are ordinarily pronounced orally immediately on close of argument. Such are some of the major differences between the two patterns.

To assert that there are distinct national patterns is not to gainsay the fact that in both countries great diversity exists from one appellate court to another. This seems inevitable in the United States, with its separate judicial systems for each of the 50 quasi-sovereign states and another for the Federal Government. But the situation is not very different in England despite its unitary, compact government. Substantial differences exist from one court to another. For example, in the Court of Criminal Appeal the judges customarily read the record of proceedings below in advance of oral argument, whereas in the Court of Appeal they do not. In the House of Lords, each judge ordinarily renders his own opinion, whereas in the Privy Council a single opinion for the entire court is prepared. In the Divisional Court of the Queen's Bench, factual determinations are not open to review, whereas in the Divisional Court of the Probate, Divorce, and Admiralty Division they are. The number of judges who sit, the way in which they go about their work, the manner in which their decisions are announced—such characteristics vary widely from one court to another, not only within the United States, but also in England.

Nevertheless, in each country a distinctive national pattern can be discerned. It is the purpose of this chapter to describe the two patterns and to compare them.

Personnel

JUDGES

(a) *Their number.* In all of England, there are only 21 judges devoting their full time to appellate work, 12 on the Court of Appeal and nine sharing their labors between the House of Lords and the Privy Council. Other appellate work, as in the Court of Criminal Appeal and the Divisional Courts of the High Court, is done by judges who devote the major share of their time to conducting trials in the first instance.[1]

In the United States, there are over 600 judges engaged exclusively in appellate work.[2] New York State alone has 34 such judges—seven on the Court of Appeals, and 27 on four departments of the Appellate Division of the Supreme Court. This does not count the federal appellate judges sitting in the state, of whom there are nine on the United States Court of Appeals for the Second Circuit, which serves the states of New York, Connecticut, and Vermont, but derives most of its business from New York. As in England, some appellate work is done by trial judges. For example, the county courts of New York hear appeals from justices of the peace, and the Appellate Term of the Supreme Court of the First Department hears appeals from the Civil Court of the City of New York (formerly the City Court and the Municipal Court). Nor is New York alone in having more appellate judges than all of England. Several other states having smaller populations exceed it in the amount of manpower devoted to appellate work.[3]

England has far fewer appeals than the United States, even in relation to the size of its population. This may be due to a smaller volume of litigation at the trial level, to greater satisfaction with the trial courts, to the discretionary refusal to review most criminal cases, to the discouragement of frivolous appeals by costs sanctions and a highly responsible bar, or to a combination of such factors. But the limited volume of appellate work for the nation as a whole does not mean that the volume of work for a particular court is small. The caseload per judge in England is not dissimilar to that found in a busy American court. For example, the United States Court of Appeals for the Second Circuit, with nine judges, decides between 350 and 400 cases a year on the merits; the English Court of Appeal, with 12 judges, decides 400 to 600 cases a year on the merits. Both courts sit in panels of three judges each. The seemingly leisurely pace of an English appeal sometimes leads casual observers to the belief that English appellate courts have little to do or that they work slowly. Either conclusion is far from the truth.

England's economy in the use of judicial manpower is due in large part to its flexibility. The appellate courts do not use their entire membership for the hearing of each appeal, but sit in divisions, which are ordinarily small though flexible in size. Thus the House of Lords, which is composed of nine Lords of Appeal in Ordinary and certain other peers who hold or have held high judicial office, ordinarily sits in a panel of five members, but the number can be as small as three, or it can be greater than five, depending upon the discretion of the Lord Chancellor. Much the same is true of the Privy Council, composed roughly of the same personnel, where the usual number of judges sitting is either three or five. The Court of Appeal is composed of 12 judges, but sits in four panels of three judges each, with all four panels in operation simultaneously. The Court of Criminal Appeal has a very fluid membership: all 34 of the Queen's Bench judges are eligible to sit, but the usual number is three. The Lord Chief Justice, who determines which particular judges are to sit on a given day, can increase this to five, seven, or even more. These

Queen's Bench judges spend part of their time trying cases in the first instance, part of it in hearing appeals, and thus remain sensitive to the kinds of problems which arise at both levels.

The position of the Lord Chief Justice illustrates the flexibility of the English system. He tries many cases in the first instance, both civil and criminal. He usually presides in the Court of Criminal Appeal, the Divisional Court of the Queen's Bench Division, and the Courts-Martial Appeal Court. He can sit, although he usually does not do so, in the Court of Appeal, the House of Lords, and the Privy Council.

The American system is more rigid. American appellate judges ordinarily do no trial work whatever, and some of them are accused of losing touch with and failing to understand the problems of trial judges. Furthermore, most appellate courts in the United States sit only en banc. Thus all nine judges of the Supreme Court of the United States and all seven judges of the New York Court of Appeals ordinarily hear every appeal. While this concentrates the attention of the entire court on every appeal, many judge-hours have to be spent in hearing arguments and studying papers, and many more in attempting to secure agreement among a large number of judges.

It is not surprising, therefore, to find that a few American appellate courts follow the English practice of sitting in divisions or panels. Thus the United States Court of Appeals for the Second Circuit, which is composed of nine judges, sits in panels of three. However, only one such panel is in operation at any one time. The other six judges are not then sitting to hear other appeals, but working on decisions in cases heard by them earlier. Similarly, in the Appellate Division, First Department, of the New York Supreme Court, five judges out of the total membership of eight sit to hear each appeal. Membership in the group varies from day to day, and the judges who are not sitting devote their time to the study of cases that previously have been heard or that are to be heard in the future. These courts, however, represent the exception rather than the rule. In most American courts, all of the judges sit to hear all of the appeals.

(b) *The manner of their selection.* In England, all appellate judges are appointed by the Crown on the recommendation either of the Lord Chancellor or the Prime Minister (acting after consultation with the Lord Chancellor). Their tenure is during good behavior, but those appointed after December 17, 1959, must retire at age 75. In the United States, federal judges are appointed by the President with the advice and consent of the Senate, and they hold office during good behavior until voluntary retirement at age 65 or 70, or later depending on length of service. State court judges may be either appointed (usually by the governor) or popularly elected. Terms of office range from a few years to life.

In England, political considerations play a very minor role in judicial appointments. For example, during his long tenure as Lord Chancellor, Lord Jowitt appointed only one member of his own party to the judiciary. In the United States, on the other hand, political considerations are extremely important, sometimes controlling. This is true even of judges who are appointed rather than elected. With rare exceptions, Republican Presidents and governors have appointed Republican judges, and Democratic Presidents and governors have appointed Democratic judges.

In England, the prestige of judicial office is so high that it is rarely refused by a practicing barrister, no matter how successful his practice or how great his income. In the United States, some of the most successful lawyers will not accept appointment to judicial office, unless to one of the relatively few "prestige" courts, like the United States Supreme Court. It is by no means unknown for an American judge to resign his office in order to reenter private practice—a course that would be regarded as shocking in England.

In England, almost all appellate judges have had previous experience as trial judges, and before that as barristers heavily engaged in litigation. In the United States, neither previous service as a trial judge nor extensive experience in litigation is regarded as a necessary qualification for appointment to an appellate bench. Not infrequently a professor of law is appointed, or an office lawyer of the type who would be called in England a solicitor.

In England, the lawyers who appear before appellate courts are few in number (less than 2,000 in the entire nation) and are generally experts in their work. These barristers are specialists not only in the art of advocacy, but also ordinarily in a particular field of law, so that a man who handles matrimonial cases is not likely to do commercial or personal injury work. Barristers are chosen to appear in particular cases by solicitors, again a limited group numbering less than 20,000. These men, who represent the other branch of the legal profession, do not ordinarily appear as advocates (in fact, they are prohibited from so acting in the High Court and in most appellate courts), but they make it their business to know which barristers are best qualified to handle particular cases. The choice of a barrister to handle an appeal (or for that matter a trial) is thus a professional, informed judgment, assuring a minimum level of competency. Since the bar is very small, and since the great majority of barristers are concentrated in London, those who appear before appellate courts tend to do so frequently, and almost always are known to the judges. Furthermore, because of the close discipline exercised over the bar by the Inns of Court and by judges, because of the ancient traditions of a proud profession, because the civil jury has virtually disappeared, and because counsel deal with those they represent through solicitors and thus rarely, if ever, become personally involved in the causes of litigants, judges are able to place great trust in the statements of the advocates who appear before them.

The English system of imposing costs on the losing party gives the judges additional assurance in advance that cases they hear are not being frivolously appealed or defended. It does not, however, operate to deprive indigent persons of their day in court simply because they are poor. That is because legal aid is highly developed in England on the appellate as well as the trial level, and for criminal as well as civil cases. But legal aid is in the hands of the bench and bar, and the cases of indigent persons no less than those of others are screened for merit before they are allowed to go to court.

The same degree of specialization and responsibility in appellate litigation does not prevail in the United States. The profession is enormously large, with the number of lawyers, all of whom are authorized to act as appellate advocates, exceeding 250,000.[4] In New York State alone there are more than twice as many lawyers as there are barristers and solicitors combined in the whole of England.[5] Any lawyer can appear in any appellate court in any kind of case if only his lay client is willing to trust him. Furthermore, there is no system of costs designed to discourage frivolous appeals. The control of the docket of an American appellate court therefore depends upon a legislative definition of the types of cases which can be appealed, or upon the exercise of discretion by the judges—generally those on the court to which the appeal is directed. The consequence is that a lawyer may appear before a given appellate court only once in his lifetime. He will probably be totally unknown to the judges, and he himself may be unfamiliar with the procedure of the court, unskilled in advocacy generally, and even unfamiliar with the type of case that he is arguing. This is one of the reasons why appellate courts sometimes feel impelled to decide cases upon grounds never mentioned or briefed by counsel.

American appellate judges ordinarily receive less help from the lawyers who appear before them than do English judges. They (and the law clerks who assist them) tend to bear the brunt of the work involved in reaching a decision, sometimes having to ferret out for themselves the crucial issues as well as the governing authorities.

The only notable exception to the general picture exists with respect to government lawyers. They ordinarily handle a large volume of litigation in a particular court with great skill and with a high sense of responsibility. For example, the Solicitor General of the United States and the lawyers in his office appear only before the United States Supreme Court. They are among the ablest advocates in the nation.

In the United States, most appellate judges have law clerks, sometimes more than one. These typically are young men, recently graduated from law school with fine academic records, who serve for a period of a year or two. They are chosen by and answerable to the judges, although paid out of public funds. The services they perform vary greatly from one judge to another, but in general they carry on research, prepare memoranda, discuss the cases to be decided with the judges for whom they work, and sometimes even draft opinions or parts of opinions to be rendered. They are particularly valuable in cases which have been inadequately presented by counsel. They participate in the decisional process to the extent that their judges wish them to participate, sometimes playing in chambers the role that advocates should, but frequently do not, play in open court, sometimes challenging and testing tentative hypotheses forming in the minds of their superiors. They have nothing to do with deciding which cases are to be published or in what form they are to appear.

In England there are no law clerks. Since typically no briefs are used, and since most opinions are rendered by the judges extemporaneously at the close of competent oral argument, it is difficult to see what use law clerks would be in most English appellate courts. But even in the House of Lords and Privy Council, where written arguments of a sort are permitted and where decisions are customarily reserved and rendered in written form, law clerks are unknown.

There are, however, a group of barristers in England who perform some of the functions performed by American law clerks. These are the law reporters. They never participate in the process of reaching a decision, but they have important duties to perform after it has been rendered. They verify names, dates, and places mentioned, check citations and improve language in much the same way that an American law clerk would work upon a draft opinion dictated by his judge. Furthermore, they are responsible to a very large extent for choosing which decisions will be published in the *Law Reports*. Since a relatively small proportion of the total number rendered are published, the law reporters and their editors have a great influence in determining the shape and content of English law for the future.[6]

The difference between the two countries in methods of rendering judgment also tends to explain the difference in the stenographic help available to English and American judges. In England no judge as such has a private secretary. He has a clerk who makes appointments, keeps papers in order, and the like, but who may not be able to act as a stenographer. This is true even in the House of Lords and the Privy Council, where decisions are customarily written out in advance: the judges have to be content with help from a secretarial pool. In America, on the other hand, almost every appellate judge has a private secretary, the theory being that it would be almost impossible for him to do his work without such assistance.

Jurisdiction

In England specialization of appellate jurisdiction is the norm. Thus the Court of Appeal handles only civil cases, the Court of Criminal Appeal only criminal cases, and the Divisional Court of the Probate, Divorce, and Admiralty Division only matrimonial cases. The pattern is varied somewhat in the House of Lords and the Privy Council, which are empowered to hear all types of appeals, but they hear so few criminal cases that they may fairly be regarded as almost wholly civil tribunals. Similarly, it is varied in the Divisional Court of the Queen's Bench, which hears appeals in petty criminal cases and reviews by means of prerogative writs the civil determinations of governmental (what in America are called "administrative") agencies. Nevertheless its jurisdiction is far from general, for the court never gets an ordinary civil case, matrimonial or otherwise, or a very serious criminal case.

In the United States, a different situation prevails. The federal Courts of Appeals and the Supreme Court, no less than the appellate courts of most states, handle criminal cases of all types as well as civil cases of all types. Judicial work loads are distributed between courts upon the basis of the geographical origin of the cases being reviewed, not upon the basis of subject matter. This is well illustrated by the organization of the United States Courts of Appeals. There are 11 such courts, each serving a different geographical area but each having the same jurisdiction as to subject matter. While the Supreme Court is specialized in the sense that it concerns itself only with federal questions, this is due to its unique position in the federal system rather than to any deliberate attempt to concentrate on any particular type of case (as distinguished from issue). The only states that follow the English pattern of separating criminal appeals from civil appeals are Oklahoma and Texas.

Appellate review of criminal cases in the United States is more frequent, but less broad in scope, than in England. In the United States, one appeal is allowed as of right from virtually every criminal trial. Further review, though often discretionary, is commonly provided, with the consequence that the highest courts of the various states and the United States Supreme Court spend a very substantial proportion of their time on criminal matters. In England, very few cases can be appealed even once as a matter of right. Ordinarily the Court of Criminal Appeal must grant leave, and it does so in not much more than ten percent of the cases in which application is made.[7] Further review in the House of Lords is extremely rare, only one or two cases a year ordinarily being allowed to go up.[8]

On the other hand, when review is allowed in England, its scope is broad. The Court of Criminal Appeal is empowered to review determinations of fact as well as determinations of law; and, even more important, to review the propriety of sentences which are within legal limits. It has power to revise sentences either up or down, and it exercises that power in such a way as to try to make the administration of criminal justice reasonably uniform throughout the nation.[9] Very few American courts have any such power. In the great majority of states and in the federal system, appellate power over sentencing is limited to the question of legality and does not extend to any control over trial court dis-

cretion. Furthermore, in many American courts the power to review convictions (as distinguished from sentences) is limited to
questions of law.

Applications for Leave to Appeal

Both in England and in the United States, appellate dockets
are to some degree within the control of the judges. In other
words, while some appeals can be taken as a matter of right, others
can be taken only by permission.

In the United States, there is usually one appeal as of right
from the trial court. After that appeal has been decided, further
review is likely to be discretionary, with leave ordinarily granted
only by the court to which the appeal is taken. Thus only the
United States Supreme Court is empowered to grant certiorari to
review the decisions of state supreme courts or federal courts of
appeals.[10] A few exceptions exist, however. Thus a federal district
court under certain circumstances may permit an appeal from an
interlocutory order made by itself to go to a court of appeals. A
somewhat similar procedure allows a federal court of appeals to
"certify" certain questions to the Supreme Court. These are unusual situations, however; ordinarily the court that renders a decision has nothing to say about whether an appeal may be taken
from it.

In England, the courts below have a greater say in determining what appeals may go up. An unsuccessful litigant in the Court
of Appeal or the Court of Criminal Appeal first applies to that
court for leave to go to the House of Lords. If the lower court
refuses, an application may be made to the House of Lords itself.[11]
Much the same procedure prevails with respect to appeals to the
Privy Council from courts in the Commonwealth countries.

A difference exists between the two countries as to the form
in which applications for leave to appeal are made. In the United
States, applications are made in writing and decided by the court
on the papers alone, without hearing oral argument. In England,
roughly the same procedure is followed by the Court of Criminal
Appeal on applications for leave to appeal from courts below it.

On applications to appeal to the House of Lords, however, the procedure is primarily oral. As soon as the Court of Appeal or the Court of Criminal Appeal announces its decision, counsel for the losing party orally asks for leave to appeal further. The case is fresh in the minds of the judges, so they can act upon it summarily. If they grant leave, the matter is disposed of without any paper work whatever. If they refuse, a written petition is presented to the House of Lords. Then comes oral argument. Counsel are permitted to appear before an Appeal Committee of the House of Lords to argue why leave should or should not be granted. These arguments ordinarily take only ten or fifteen minutes each, and, upon their conclusion, the judges announce their decision. Substantially the same procedure is followed on appeals to the Privy Council.

Papers on Appeal

An outstanding difference between the two nations is the fact that briefs are required in the United States, whereas in England they are not. The brief is a full-dress argument in writing, often running 50 or more printed or mimeographed pages in length. It states the facts, outlines the claimed errors in the proceedings below, and cites and discusses the authorities claimed to justify reversal or affirmance. The appellant serves his brief on the other side well in advance of the time for oral argument, and the respondent then serves his answering brief on the appellant, again well in advance of oral argument. Sometimes the appellant serves a reply brief.

In England such a document is virtually unknown. The closest approach to it is the "case" normally required from both sides in the House of Lords and Privy Council. This, however, is a very abbreviated paper, seldom running more than six or seven pages in length, and is intended only as a preliminary outline of the extended oral argument to be made later. It does not discuss authorities in detail, or argue the propositions of law to be relied upon. Relatively few cases are cited (although this may be attributable more to the English theory of precedent than to the form which papers on appeal take). In the other appellate courts of England, no written arguments of any kind are used.

In both England and the United States, the judges are furnished with a record on appeal. It consists of the notice of appeal, pleadings, and other formal documents, the judgment below, and so much of the evidence as may be relevant as to the questions raised on appeal. There is this difference, however: English appellate courts are almost always provided at the outset of their deliberations with a helpful bird's-eye view of the case and the issues to be resolved. In a case tried without a jury—the typical civil case—this takes the form of a reasoned, though often extemporaneous, opinion by the judge below. It outlines the evidence, the authorities relied upon, the decision and the reasons therefor. In a criminal case or in one of the few civil cases tried by jury, the judge's charge to the jury serves the same purpose. It ordinarily summarizes the evidence as well as the law and often expresses the judge's opinion on the merits as well. In the United States, equivalent trial aids to appellate review are usually lacking. If the case has been tried by jury, as a great many civil and almost all criminal cases are, the judge's instructions usually consist of little more than abstract propositions of law, without any summary of or comment upon the evidence. If the case has been tried without a jury, there are ordinarily only formalized findings of fact and conclusions of law, without the citation of authorities. Sometimes there is a reasoned opinion below, as when the case has gone through an intermediate stage of appeal, but this is the exception rather than the rule.

In England, the record on appeal is almost always mimeographed. In the United States, it often has to be printed at great expense. The practice, however, varies from one court to another, some courts permitting mimeographing or other relatively cheap forms of duplication.

Oral Argument

In the United States, oral arguments are secondary in importance to briefs and are rigidly limited in duration. In the

United States Supreme Court, one hour is allowed to each side, but in many appellate courts less time than that is permitted, frequently no more than 15 minutes or a half hour for each side. Reading by counsel is frowned upon. The judges do not wish to hear what they can read for themselves. They expect to get all the information they need about the judgment below, the evidence, and the authorities relied upon from studying the briefs and record on appeal. They do not encourage counsel to discuss in detail the precedents claimed to govern the decision, preferring to do that job by themselves in the relative privacy of their chambers, often with the assistance of law clerks.

In England, where there are no written briefs, oral arguments are all-important. They are never arbitrarily limited in duration. While some last for only a few minutes, others go on for many days, even weeks. The average duration of a case in the Court of Appeal is a day and a quarter. Much of the time, perhaps half, is spent by counsel reading aloud to the court. It is in this way that the judges learn what transpired in the court below (by listening to a reading of the judgment and such parts of the evidence as may be relevant), what errors are complained of by counsel (by listening to a reading of the notice of appeal, which is required to specify the errors), and the authorities relied on by counsel (by listening to a reading of statutes and cases, either in their entirety or in large part). There are some departures from this pattern, notably in the Court of Criminal Appeal,[12] and attempts are now being made in other English courts to cut down the amount of time spent in reading by counsel,[13] but the general picture is as stated.

The only controls ordinarily exercised in England over the time of oral argument are informal, ad hoc suggestions from the judges. Thus when counsel wishes to cite a case as authority, the presiding judge may ask him: for what proposition? If the judges indicate that they accept the proposition as stated, there is no need to read the case. Similarly, if counsel has persuaded the judges on a certain point, they may indicate that it is unnecessary for him to pursue it further. If counsel for the appellant, by the time he finishes his argument, has failed to persuade the court that the decision below should be reversed or modified, the court informs counsel for the respondent that it does not wish to hear from him at all, and proceeds forthwith to deliver judgment. Despite such controls as these, the time spent in England in oral argument is very much greater than that spent in the United States.

Many observers, including a large number of American judges, believe that the quality of appellate advocacy in the United States is low, and that it is declining. If they are correct, a partial explanation may lie in the fact that rigid time limitations allow little opportunity for its development. Another partial explanation may be the fact that oral argument is regarded as relatively unimportant as compared to written argument. Indeed, in some courts oral argument is rarely heard, and in others it tends to become hardly more than ritual (especially when the judges have not read the briefs in advance).

The Decision

In the United States, virtually all decisions are reserved and rendered in written form. Rarely is one pronounced from the bench.[14] Furthermore, an attempt is always made to have the judges agree upon an opinion for the court as a whole, or, if that cannot be done, to secure as broad a base of agreement as possible. While concurring opinions are not unusual, and even multiple separate dissents not unknown, it is not expected that each judge will express his own views. The ideal is a unanimous opinion for the court, or failing that, one majority opinion and one dissent.

In England, few decisions are either reserved or written. In the Court of Appeal, the practice is for each judge to express his individual views orally and extemporaneously immediately upon the close of argument. In the Court of Criminal Appeal, a single opinion for the court is customarily announced, but usually orally and extemporaneously. Only in the House of Lords and the Privy Council are decisions customarily reserved and written.

The American approach entails internal operating procedures different from those that are usual in England. Conferences, both formal and informal, are a prominent feature of American practice. So are exchanges of memoranda and draft opinions. On the other hand, since reading and writing are by their nature solitary operations, American judges—who are compelled to do much of both—spend many, if not most, of their working hours alone. They are frequently required to shift their attention from one case to another and then back again because, with cases being heard in batches, several are awaiting decision at any given time.

To the limited extent that the English practice conforms to the American pattern, the same internal procedures doubtless apply. In the great majority of English appeals, however, the judges follow a vastly different routine. Most of their working time is spent sitting together on the bench, listening and talking rather than reading and writing. The discussions they hold are brief and seemingly casual, although highly economical, by reason of the fact that cases are heard and decided one at a time. The judges' minds are already focused on the problems at hand and are not distracted by other cases which have been heard and are awaiting decision. They whisper between themselves on the bench, they converse as they walk to and from the courtroom, and they indirectly make comments to each other as they carry on Socratic dialogues with counsel. But they do not ordinarily exchange memoranda or draft opinions or engage in full-scale conferences.

In short, the appellate judge in England spends most of his working time in open court, relatively little in chambers, whereas his counterpart in America spends most of his working time in chambers, and relatively little in open court. This is neatly illustrated by the times of sitting for comparable courts in the two nations. In the United States Court of Appeals for the Second Circuit, each judge hears arguments one week out of four, and uses the other three for studying briefs and records on appeal, conferring with his brother judges, and writing opinions. In contrast, each judge on the English Court of Appeal hears arguments from 10:30 A.M. to 1 P.M. and from 2 P.M. to 4:15 P.M. day after day, five days a week, throughout each term.

Although English judges spend more time in the courtroom on each case, American judges probably spend more total time on each case—reading briefs, hearing arguments, doing research, conferring with their brother judges and their law clerks, and writing opinions. Many of the same intellectual labors that American judges perform episodically on and off the bench are performed by English judges in concentrated form on the bench.

English appellate procedure, however leisurely it may appear on the surface, is not dilatory. In civil cases heard by the Court of Appeal, the average time that elapses between the filing of the notice of appeal and the decision is about six months. In cases heard by the Court of Criminal Appeal, the average time is about one month. In a roughly comparable American court—the United States Court of Appeals for the Second Circuit—the average time for both civil and criminal cases is about nine months. This is not out of line with other appellate courts in the United States.[15]

Precedent

In the United States, an appellate court is free to overrule its own previous decisions. In England it is not, and corrective action must come through legislation. In this sense, the United States seems to have a far less rigid doctrine of precedent than England.

In another sense, however, English judges are freer than American judges to decide cases as they feel that justice demands. That is because the bulk of English case law is slight as compared to the bulk of American case law. English case law grows very slowly,[16] whereas American case law grows at the rate of hundreds of volumes a year.

Cases produced by the federal courts of the United States (these are of potential significance to every court in the land, state and local as well as federal) fill about 25 volumes a year. In a single large state like New York, there may be an almost equal flood of reported cases, far exceeding the number produced in all of England. Many of the cases are primarily factual determinations which do not enunciate new principles of law or alter or modify existing principles. Nevertheless they may be, and frequently are, cited as precedents for future cases. This restricts the freedom of action of judges, for they are called upon to compare minutely the fact patterns in previous cases with the one before them in order to avoid treating one litigant differently from another. If they were free merely to interpret and apply broad statements of general principle they would not be hemmed in to the extent that they are.

Other consequences flow from the sheer bulk of American precedent. The costs of litigation are increased, not only in terms of the expense of reports, digests, indexes, and texts, but also in terms of the time spent by lawyers and judges in poring over them. The citation of cases tends to become a habit, almost an obsession, with dozens of cases being cited where one would do, or even where the proposition for which they stand is so obvious that no one disputes it. There is also the grave danger that even competent and conscientious judges and lawyers may overlook important cases in the welter of reports, already so numerous as to be almost unmanageable. Despite restatements of the law, and despite even the development of electronic data-retrieval machines, the difficulty of separating the wheat from the chaff grows constantly more critical.

In England, the situation is markedly different. Few cases are available to be cited. Only about 75 percent of those decided by the House of Lords and Privy Council, 25 percent of those decided by the Court of Appeal, and 10 percent of those decided by the Court of Criminal Appeal are published. Even so, some judges and lawyers complain that there are too many reports. The English theory is that only decisions which enunciate principles of law have precedent value. Ones which only apply well-settled principles to specific fact situations are not considered worthy of preservation in the *Law Reports*. The selection of cases to be published is made primarily by the law reporters and their editors.[17]

Another characteristic of English precedents is that there are often several opinions in each case, from which a *ratio* for the case at hand may be chosen. This comes from the practice of each judge in the House of Lords, the Court of Appeal, and the divisional courts expressing his own views rather than joining in a common opinion.

The consequence of the English system of rendering and publishing decisions is that the common law of England, while highly manageable, is not very specific. To a considerable extent, it is truly "unwritten" and carried largely in the heads of the judges and lawyers. The judges have reasonably clean slates upon which to write.

Statutory Interpretation

In both nations, much of the work of appellate courts consists in the interpretation of statutes.

In England, the approach tends to be literal. Increasingly, great emphasis is being placed upon the precise words used by Parliament because statutes tend to be drafted in greater and greater detail. The courts make no use of committee reports or parliamentary debates to aid their understanding of the objectives of the legislation being construed. They rarely discuss even in general terms the policy behind a statute.

In the United States, a literal approach to statutory interpretation is not favored. If legislative history is available to illuminate the purpose of legislation, as in committee reports or legislative debates, the courts make free use of it. If it is not available (as is usually the case with respect to state statutes), they look at the evil aimed at by the legislature as well as the words used by it to correct that evil.

Conception of Role

In England, appellate judges tend to regard their job as complete when they reach a correct conclusion on the case presented to them. They are inclined to worry less than American judges about the effect of their decisions as precedents. They cannot even be sure that they will ever be published in the *Law Reports*. Even if they know that a particular decision will be published, they may be content to leave its ultimate published form primarily to the law reporters. Furthermore, they are so imbued with the idea of the supremacy of Parliament that they do not think much about their own lawmaking functions.

This is not to suggest that English judges are not conscious of their interstitial lawmaking, or that they are not expert at distinguishing earlier cases. They have developed that art to a high degree, and have been careful to keep it an art, for the rules for discovering the *ratio decedendi* of an earlier decision have never been authoritatively laid down. But the central fact remains that they conceive their role modestly. They do not over-rule prior decisions, they do not invalidate statutes (they have no written constitution and no doctrine of judicial supremacy), and they do not decide cases upon grounds or authorities not urged by counsel. For the reasons suggested, an appeal is regarded not as something apart, but as a sort of extension of trial, with the appellate judges doing their work in open court in a manner and with a motivation not greatly different from that of trial judges. Symptomatic of this attitude are these facts: (1) in both the Court of Appeal and the Court of Criminal Appeal, it is possible for the court to take new evidence; (2) both courts re-view questions of fact as well as questions of law; (3) the Court of Criminal Appeal reviews the propriety as well as the legality of sentences; (4) litigants are very often present at the argument of an appeal, especially in the Court of Criminal Appeal, where the accused ordinarily has a right to be present.

In the United States, the appellate process is accorded greater prominence than in England. It is treated as something quite distinct from the trial process, and, in a sense, something vastly more important. Appellate judges are ordinarily assured of the publication of every opinion they write. They usually need not concern themselves directly with litigants, or even with questions of fact, but may concentrate on questions of law and policy. Their work sometimes seems more akin to that of research scholars than that of trial judges. Insofar as they deal with constitutional prob-lems, they are dealing with matters beyond even the reach of ordi-nary legislative processes. Insofar as they deal with statutory or common-law problems, many judges conceive it to be their duty to reform rules that they consider unjust or obsolete. They place greater stress on their lawmaking functions than do their English cousins, being at least as interested in laying down guidelines for the future as in deciding correctly the cases before them.

Finality

In England, appeals terminate litigation, subject only to the possibility of further review in a higher court or a retrial in the court below. Rehearings are not permitted, and even new trials are prohibited in criminal cases. The idea is carried to such an extent that if an error that the reviewing court cannot classify as harmless is found in a criminal trial, the court has no alternative but to quash the conviction and set the accused free, even though there may be no genuine doubt as to his guilt.[18]

There is no federal system in England to create conflicts between different jurisdictions and thus permit successive applications for the same relief to different tribunals, nor is there any expansion of the writ of habeas corpus or any similar remedy in such a way as to allow the reexamination of judgments rendered by legally constituted tribunals acting within their jurisdiction.

Finally, the English doctrine of precedent is sufficiently rigid to render pointless any relitigation of a question once unequivocally decided. If a citizen is unhappy about the law, he had better seek corrective action in Parliament rather than squander his wealth on hopeless litigation.

In the United States, appellate decisions possess less finality. New trials can be granted in all types of cases, criminal as well as civil. Rehearings are frequently asked and occasionally allowed. Existing side by side with appeals are a variety of methods of collateral attack, including habeas corpus, sometimes entailing successive reexaminations of a single case by courts of coordinate jurisdiction.

Finally, the American doctrine of precedent is such that a decision is never beyond the reach of challenge in a new lawsuit. If conditions or thinking have changed—sometimes if only the personnel of the court has changed—there is always the possibility that the unwanted decision may be overruled. When that happens, as it does fairly frequently, still more litigation may be engendered, sometimes on a grand scale. The overruling decision, necessarily limited to the problem presented in the particular litigation, may raise many new problems that, not being before the court and not being provided for by legislative enactment, will have to be resolved in later cases. Thus some of the landmark decisions of American law seem less to have solved problems than to have created them. The school-segregation decision,[19] the reapportionment decision,[20] and the school-prayer decision [21] are cases in point.

NOTES

Chapter 2

1. [1959–60] N.Y. Judicial Conference, 6th Ann. Rep., Table IV, at 207 (1961); N.Y. Const. art. 6, § 2; N.Y. Judiciary Law § 140; N.Y. Judiciary Law §§ 70, 140 (McKinney Supp. 1962).

2. Supreme Court, N.Y. Civ. Prac. Act, §§ 608–11; Surrogate Court, N.Y. Surr. Ct. Act § 288; Family Court, N.Y. Family Ct. Act § 1011 (McKinney, Court Reorganization Acts of 1962).

3. N.Y. Const. art. VI, §§ 8, 34(a) (McKinney Supp. 1962); N.Y. Civ. Prac. Act § 623; N.Y. App. Div. (1st Dep't) R. 10. Civil Court, Civil Ct. of the City of N.Y. Act § 136 (McKinney, Court Reorganization Acts of 1962); N.Y. App. Term (1st Dep't) R. I, VI.

4. Criminal Ct. of the City of N.Y. Act § 43 (McKinney, Court Reorganization Acts of 1962). N.Y. Code Crim. Proc. §§ 519, 520. N.Y. Const. art. VI, § 8(d); N.Y. App. Term (1st Dep't) Rules, as amended June 28, 1962.

5. N.Y. Civ. Prac. Act §§ 557, 608 (final judgment), §§ 609, 610 (order in action), § 611 (interlocutory judgment). See 9 Carmody-Wait, Encyclopedia of New York Practice 495–514 (1954).

6. In addition to its appellate jurisdiction, which accounts for the main bulk of its work, the Appellate Division has some original and administrative jurisdiction not of present concern. Thus it handles disciplinary proceedings against lawyers (N.Y. Judiciary Law § 90; N.Y. App. Div. [1st Dep't] Special Rules Regulating Conduct of Attorneys), and judges of lower courts (Code Crim. Proc. § 132 [McKinney Supp. 1962]); reviews determinations of administrative agencies (N.Y. Civ. Prac. Act § 1296); decides controversies submitted on agreed statements of fact (N.Y. Civ. Prac. Act §§ 546–48); conducts investigations into "ambulance chasing" and

the like (N.Y. Judiciary Law § 90; N.Y. App. Div. [1st Dep't] Special Rules Regulating Conduct of Attorneys); makes certain rules of procedure and recommends certain others (N.Y. Judiciary Law §§ 83–85; N.Y. App. Div. [1st Dep't] Rules); admits attorneys to practice (N.Y. Judiciary Act §§ 90, 460; N.Y.R. Civ. Prac. 1); makes assignments of Supreme Court justices (N.Y. Const. art. VI, § 2; N.Y. Judiciary Law § 86); appoints not only its own supporting personnel (N.Y. Judiciary Law §§ 90, 460; N.Y.R. Civ. Prac. 1) but also county clerks in Manhattan and the Bronx (N.Y. Const. art. IX, § 5; N.Y. County Law § 908) and official referees (N.Y. Judiciary Law §§ 116, 116[2]); and fixes its own budget (beyond the power of veto) (N.Y. Judiciary Law § 86).

7. Code Crim. Proc. § 517.

8. Code Crim. Proc. § 518.

9. The normal complement is seven justices. An eighth justice is now serving by special designation of the governor because of the court's heavy caseload. He does not have a regular five-year term, but, in all other respects, is like any other associate justice.

10. N.Y. Const. art. VI, § 4.

11. N.Y. Const. art. VI, § 2; N.Y. Judiciary Law §§ 141, 144; N.Y. Legislative Ann. 1961–62, at 868.

12. *Ibid.* The presiding justices of the four departments of the Appellate Division play a key role in allocating the judicial manpower of the state to the courts where needed.

13. N.Y. Judiciary Law §§ 210 et seq.

14. [1959–60] N.Y. Judicial Conference, 6th Ann. Rep., Table IV, at 207 (1961).

15. *Id.* Table III.

16. *Ibid.*

17. N.Y. App. Div. (1st Dep't) R. VI-A; N.Y.R. Civ. Prac. 234.

18. N.Y. App. Div. (1st Dep't) R. V.

19. *Ibid.*

20. *Ibid.*

21. N.Y.R. Civ. Prac. 234; N.Y. App. Div. (1st Dep't) R. VI.

22. N.Y.R. Civ. Prac. 235; N.Y. App. Div. (1st Dep't), Special Rules (record and briefs).

23. N.Y. Civ. Prac. Act § 558.

24. Willcox, Karlen & Roemer, Justice Lost—By What Appellate Papers Cost, 33 N.Y.U.L. Rev. 934 (1958).

25. N.Y. App. Div. (1st Dep't) R. V, VI.

26. *Ibid.* N.Y.R. Civ. Prac. 234; N.Y. Civ. Prac. Act §§ 612, 632.

27. N.Y. App. Div. (1st Dep't) R. VI.

28. N.Y. App. Div. (1st Dep't) R. VI.

29. "During [1949] the court decided 1,239 appeals. If we assume that the briefs and records on appeal consumed the modest amount of only 350 pages per case, the total number of printed pages with which the court was confronted would be 433,650. Since five judges sat on each case, and since there were a total of seven judges for the entire Appellate Division, First Department, each justice would be responsible for approximately five-sevenths of that reading material or a total of 309,750 pages. Even superior readers, reading for relatively short periods, dealing with merely college level material and satisfied with 80 per cent comprehension, average only 340 words per minute. If such reading could be sustained for as long a period as one hour, 68 pages could be covered.

"If each judge, operating at that fantastic rate of speed, read every record in its entirety as well as every brief in every case in which he participated, it would take him 4,555 hours. That would be more than twelve hours per day for 365 days of the year, including Saturdays, Sundays and holidays. The time so spent would be exclusive of time spent in preparing for and sitting in conference (all day almost every Monday during court terms), listening to arguments (10 afternoons per month on an average), writing opinions (there were 250 written in 1949), deciding motions (there were 1,226 in 1949), doing administrative work, etc."

Karlen, Cost of Appeals Study, Institute of Judicial Administration, Jan. 15, 1954.

30. Shientag, The Appellate Division, First Department, Its Jurisdiction, How It Functions in Conference, Briefs and Oral Arguments Presented to It, 5 Record of N.Y.C.B.A. 377 (1950).

31. Shientag, *op. cit.,* at 401.

32. [1959–60] N.Y. Judicial Conference, 6th Ann. Rep., Table V, at 208 (1961).

33. These figures include opinions on disciplinary and other nonappellate proceedings.

34. N.Y. App. Div. (1st Dep't) R. VIII.

Chapter 3

1. N.Y. Const. art. VI, §§ 2, 3, 7.

2. Cuomo, The New York Court of Appeals; A Practical Perspective, 34 St. John's L. Rev. 197 (1960).

3. N.Y. Civ. Prac. Act §§ 588–90.

4. N.Y. Civ. Prac. Act § 589.

5. N.Y. Const. art. VI, § 3; N.Y. Code Crim. Proc. §§ 517–20 (McKinney 1962).

6. N.Y. Civ. Prac. Act § 588.

7. Cf. 6 N.Y. Jud. Conference Annual Rep. 173, 206 (1961).

8. N.Y. Ct. App. R. VII.

9. Cuomo, *supra* note 2, at 202.

10. Cuomo, *supra* note 2, at 207, 211.

11. *Id.* at 204.

12. See Chief Judge Andrew's opinion in Sciolina v. Erie Preserving Co., 151 N.Y. 50, 45 N.E. 371 (1896).

13. Cohen & Karger, Powers of the New York Court of Appeals, § 82, at 355 (rev. ed. 1952).

14. N.Y. Judiciary Law § 23.

15. 45 Jour. Am. Jud. Soc. 333 et seq.

16. *Id.*

17. N.Y. Judiciary Law § 210.

18. N.Y. Const. art. VI, § 28.

19. Cohen & Karger, *supra* note 14, § 1, at 7.

20. The only other exception is in civil cases where the appellate division on reversing or modifying a judgment makes new findings of fact and a final determination is rendered "pursuant thereto." N.Y. Const. art. VI, § 3.

21. Loewinthan v. Le Vine, 299 N.Y. 372, 87 N.E. 2d 303 (1949).

22. In New York, as in many states, however, legislative history is sparse with respect to state statutes.

23. N.Y. Civ. Prac. Act § 558.

24. Willcox, Karlen & Roemer, Justice Lost—By What Appellate Papers Cost, 33 N.Y.U.L. Rev. 934 (1958).

25. N.Y. Ct. App. R. VII.

26. Cuomo, *supra* note 2, at 207.

27. *Ibid.*

28. Hiscock, Some Features of the Organization and Work of the Court of Appeals, 27 Cornell L. Q. 313 (1942), at 314.

29. Cuomo, *supra* note 2, at 213.

30. Crane, Minutes of the Court of Appeals, 278 N.Y. V (1938).

31. Cuomo, *supra* note 2, at 216–17.

32. *Ibid.*

33. *Ibid.*

34. *Id.* at 218.

35. 10 Buffalo L. Rev. 256 (1960).

36. *Ibid.*

37. Erie Railroad v. Tompkins, 304 U.S. 64 (1938).

38. Pennoyer v. Neff, 95 U.S. 714, 24 L.Ed. 565 (1877); Fauntleroy v. Lum, 210 U.S. 230, 28 S.Ct. 641, 52 L.Ed. 1039 (1908).

39. Brennan, Federal Habeas Corpus and State Prisoners: An Exercise in Federalism, 7 Utah L. Rev. 423 (1961).

Chapter 4

1. There are eleven judicial circuits in the nation. Except for the one covering only the District of Columbia, each circuit embraces several contiguous states.

In addition to hearing appeals from district courts, the Court of Appeals also reviews determinations made by certain federal administrative agencies and special courts—a topic not of immediate concern here. It also exercises original jurisdiction by writs of mandamus and prohibition.

2. 28 U.S.C. §33. One district (the Southern District of New York) has 24 judges.

3. Unless a case enters the federal judicial system at the trial court level—either by being brought originally in a district court or by being removed to it from a state court prior to trial (28 U.S.C. § 1441)—it stays in the state court system where brought until final review has been accomplished within that system. Thereafter, there is a possibility of federal review, but only in the United States Supreme Court.

   Indirectly, however, the Court of Appeals reviews state criminal cases when they result in habeas corpus proceedings in federal district courts and the rulings in such proceedings are appealed.

4. 18 U.S.C. §§ 875, 1201.

5. 18 U.S.C. § 2421.

6. Title 18 U.S.C. generally and section 13 in particular: "Laws of States Adopted for Areas Within Federal Jurisdiction: Whoever within or upon any of the places now existing or hereafter reserved or acquired as provided in section 7 of this title, is guilty of any act or omission which, although not made punishable by any enactment of Congress, would be punishable if committed or omitted within the jurisdiction of the State, Territory, Possession, or District in which such place is situated, by the laws thereof in force at the time of such act or omission, shall be guilty of a like offense and subject to a like punishment."

7. Here again it must be remembered that Congress cannot legislate generally in the field of torts, contracts, property, etc., but must confine itself to the limited areas entrusted to the Federal Government in the Constitution, dealing only with such matters as torts arising in interstate commerce or admiralty, patents, copyrights, bankruptcy, and federal taxes.

8. In all "diversity" cases, and in most "federal question" cases, the amount in controversy must exceed $10,000 to gain access to a federal court. 28 U.S.C. §§ 1331, 1332. Otherwise, such cases must go to state courts which are required to apply federal law wherever applicable. Second Employers' Liability Cases, 223 U.S. 1, 32 S.Ct. 169, 56 L.Ed. 327 (1911).

9. Erie R.R. v. Tompkins, 304 U.S. 64, 58 S.Ct. 817, 82 L.Ed. 1188 (1938).

10. 28 U.S.C. § 1291. Where, however, direct review in the United States Supreme Court is permitted, an appeal can be taken only to that Court.

11. 28 U.S.C. § 1292(a).

12. 28 U.S.C. § 1292(b).

13. In the course of reviewing such a decision, however, the Court may consider any interlocutory ruling that affects the final outcome. Victor Talking Machine Co. v. George, 105 F.2d 697 (CA 3, 1939).

14. 28 U.S.C. § 48. Some United States Courts of Appeals sit at various places in their circuits. Thus the Court for the Ninth Circuit, covering the states of Alaska, Hawaii, Washington, Oregon, California, Nevada, Montana, Idaho, and Arizona sits at San Francisco, Los Angeles, Portland, and Seattle.

15. Until 1961, the court had only six judges, a number which had remained constant since 1939.

16. 28 U.S.C. § 44.

17. 28 U.S.C. § 371.

18. 28 U.S.C. § 44.

19. Presently serving as senior judges are Thomas W. Swan, Carroll C. Hincks, and Harold Medina. From 1951 until his death in 1961, Learned Hand served as a senior judge.

20. 28 U.S.C. § 45.

21. 28 U.S.C. § 332.

22. 28 U.S.C. § 331.

23. More exact figures for the year ending June 30, 1960, can be found in 1960 Annual Report of Dir. of Admin. Office of the U.S. Courts, p. 211.

24. The fact that each judge participated, on the average, in less than half of the cases decided by the court is explained by the use of senior and specially assigned judges.

25. 1960 Annual Report of Dir. of Admin. Office of the U.S. Courts, pp. 210–13.

26. In an equivalent period, the Appellate Division, First Department, disposed of 1,093 appeals. Since five out of seven judges participated in each appeal, the caseload per judge averaged 780 appeals per year.

27. 1960 Annual Report of Dir. of Admin. Office of the U.S. Courts, pp. 224, 252, 288, 304.

28. By "value judgments" are meant those mental operations involved in deciding such "mixed questions of law and fact" as whether a particular time interval is "reasonable."

29. Fed. R. Civ. Pro. 52.

30. Motions are required to be in writing according to the court's own Rule 19.

31. Fed. R. Civ. Pro. 73 (normally 30 days in civil cases); Fed. R. Crim. Pro. 37 (10 days in criminal cases).

32. Assignments of error are abolished by Fed. R. Civ. Pro. 75. However, if the appellant does not designate for inclusion in the record of appeal (prepared by the clerk of the district court and transmitted to the appellate court) all of the evidence and papers in the court below, he is required to serve on the appellee "a concise statement of the points on which he intends to rely in the appeal." (Rule 75[d].)

33. Rule 17 of the court's own rules provides little guidance as to the matters to be included or their arrangement.

34. The court's own Rules 15 and 17.

35. The transcript is ordered from the court reporter and paid for by the appellant. He furnishes the copy which the clerk of the district court transmits to the Court of Appeals.

36. Fed. R. Civ. Pro. 73, 75, 76; Fed. R. Crim. Pro. 39.

37. The court's own Rule 15.

38. A joint appendix is possible (the court's own Rule 15[d]) but not used very often.

39. The court's own Rules 15 and 17.

40. The court's own Rules 15 and 17.

41. In this respect, the court is out of line with the majority of appellate courts in the United States. Willcox, Karlen & Roemer, Justice Lost—By What Appellate Papers Cost, 33 N.Y.U.L. Rev. 934 (1958). However, the requirement of printing is tempered by the use of appendices to the brief instead of a separate record on appeal. In this respect, the Second Circuit Court is in advance of many American appellate courts.

42. The court's own Rule 15.

43. The court's own Rule 15.

44. 1960 Report of Dir. of Admin. Office of the U.S. Courts, p. 221.

45. Until a few years ago, this was not so. The old practice was to call a group of cases at the beginning of a sitting without any clear idea of how much time each would consume. Counsel sometimes had to await their turn for days.

46. For earlier figures, see 1960 Report of Dir. of Admin. Office of the U.S. Courts, p. 221.

47. The court's own Rule 25.

48. The Court of Appeals may also on its own initiative certify questions to the Supreme Court, 28 U.S.C. § 1254(3). This procedure, however, is little used.

49. 29 U.S. Law Week at 3026.

Chapter 5

1. In addition to ordinary federal courts, operating in a limited sphere concurrently with state courts, there are some in the District of Columbia, the federal territories, and the Commonwealth of Puerto Rico which possess more general jurisdiction. For practical purposes, they may be regarded as the equivalent of state courts. Their decisions are ultimately subject to review in the Supreme Court on substantially the same basis as state-court decisions.

2. The Court also possesses limited original jurisdiction, 28 U.S.C. § 1251, not of present concern.

3. This term is used generally to include the highest appellate court in each state. Some such courts go by different names—for example, "Court of Appeals" in New York.

4. 28 U.S.C. § 1252. Ordinarily, appeals lie only to the United States Courts of Appeal.

5. Thompson v. City of Louisville, 362 U.S. 199 (1960).

6. These are estimates based upon statistics in The Supreme Court, 1959 Term, 74 Harv. L. Rev. 97, 100 (1960) and in 73 Harv. L. Rev. 84 (1959).

7. Second Employers Liability Cases, 223 U.S. 1 (1911).

8. See general description in paper on United States Court of Appeals for the Second Circuit.

9. Erie R.R. v. Tompkins, 304 U.S. 64 (1938). Needless to say, each state has its own statutes and its own judge-made law. A Virginia decision has no binding force in New York except insofar as the particular judgment is sought to be enforced in that state. As a mere precedent, it is only persuasive.

10. Lynch v. New York *ex. rel.* Pierson, 293 U.S. 52 (1934).

11. In Mapp v. Ohio, 367 U.S. 643 (1961), the Court discovered in the course of oral argument that counsel for the appellant did not know relevant and controlling prior decisions.

12. 28 U.S.C. §§ 1254–57; for history, see dissenting opinion of Frankfurter, J. in Dick v. New York Life Ins. Co. 359 U.S. 437, 447 (1959).

13. These bear little resemblance to their common-law forebears.

14. Sup. Ct. R. 19.

15. See, for example, Taft, The Jurisdiction of the Supreme Court Under the Act of February 13, 1925, 35 Yale L.J. 1, 2 (1925); Mr. Justice Stone in a dissent joined by Mr. Justice Brandeis: Washington Fidelity National Ins. Co. v. Burton, 287 U.S. 97, 100, 101–102 (1932); Vinson, The Business of Judicial Administration: Suggestions to the Conference of Chief Justices, 35 A.B.A.J. 893 (1949); Grier, J. in Newell v. Norton, 70 U.S. (3 Wall.) 257 (1866); Houston Oil Co. of Texas v. Goodrich, 245 U.S. 440 (1918); Lau Ou Bew v. United States, 144 U.S. 47 (1892).

16. Based on Table II, The Supreme Court, 1959 Term, 74 Harv. L. Rev. 97, at 99 (1960).

17. The excerpting is done by one of the Chief Justice's law clerks. Hart, The Time Chart of the Justices, 73 Harv. L. Rev. 85, at 90 (1959).

18. "Certiorari was granted, according to our practice, because at least four members of the Court deemed [the case] . . . 'special and important.'" Rice v. Sioux City Memorial Park Cemetery, Inc. 349 U.S. 70, 74 (1955).

19. Maryland v. Baltimore Radio Show, 338 U.S. 912 (1950); Agoston v. Pennsylvania, 340 U.S. 844 (1950).

20. Brown, Forward: Process of Law, The Supreme Court 1957, 72 Harv. L. Rev. 77 (1958).

21. Frankfurter, J., dissenting in Dick v. New York Life Ins. Co., 359 U.S. 437, 447–63 (1959), and in Ferguson v. Moore-McCormack Lines, Inc. 352 U.S. 521, 524–48 (1957).

22. Chief Justice Taft's expression in hearings before the Committee on the Judiciary of the House of Representatives on H.R. 10479, 67th Cong., 2d Sess. § 2.

23. 28 U.S.C. § 1254(2).

24. 28 U.S.C. § 1257. Some direct appeals are also allowed from district-court decisions, 28 U.S.C. 1253.

25. Sup. Ct. R. 13(2), 15.

26. Sup. Ct. R. 16.

27. Mr. Justice Brennan in Ohio *ex. rel.* Eaton v. Price, 360 U.S. 246 (1959).

28. Based on Table I, The Supreme Court, 1951 Term, 74 Harv. L. Rev. 97, 99 (1960).

29. 28 U.S.C. § 1 (1958). The office of Chief Justice is a separate office to which a man must be specially appointed. It does not rotate, nor is it reached by virtue of seniority.

30. Despite the importance of nonlegal factors in appointment, they have rarely if ever substantially affected a Justice's work on the Court. The principal historian of the Court has remarked: "Nothing is more striking in the history of the Court than the manner in which the hopes of those who expected a Judge to follow the political views of the President appointing him have been disappointed." 1 Warren, The Supreme Court in United States History 21–22.

31. Technically "during good behavior."

32. 28 U.S.C. § 371. Thereafter they may serve on lower federal courts to the extent they desire, making arrangements therefor with the chief judges of the courts concerned.

33. 28 U.S.C. § 5.

34. 28 U.S.C. § 331. This body is charged with: (1) "making a comprehensive survey of the condition of business in the courts of the U.S. and preparing plans for assignment of judges to or from circuits or districts where necessary, and [submitting] suggestions to the various courts, in the interest of uniformity and expedition of business"; (2) carrying on "a continuous study of the operation and

effect of the general rules of practice and procedure now or hereafter in use as prescribed by the Supreme Court for the other courts of the U.S. pursuant to law"; (3) recommending through the Chief Justice to the Congress in the form of an annual report of the proceedings of the Judicial Conference, its suggestions for legislation.

35. 28 U.S.C. § 604. This is the "housekeeping" organization for the United States courts.

36. 28 U.S.C. § 2. All of the justices have their chambers in the Supreme Court building, so that access between them is easy for purposes of discussion.

37. Dick v. New York Life Ins. Co. 359 U.S. 437 (1959).

38. Rogers v. Missouri P.R. Co., 352 U.S. 500 (1957); Dice v. Akron, C. & Y. R.R. 342 U.S. 359 (1952.)

39. 313 U.S. 33, 50 (1941). See also Douglas, Stare Decisis, 49 Colum. L. Rev. 735 (1949).

40. 356 U.S. 165 (1958).

41. 288 U.S. 344, 359 (1933). See also note 39 *supra*.

42. Sup. Ct. R. 17, 26.

43. Sup. Ct. R. 36.

44. Sup. Ct. R. 53.

45. Sup. Ct. R. 36.

46. Sup. Ct. R. 39, 40, 41.

47. Sup. Ct. R. 22.

48. Sup. Ct. R. 24.

49. Sup. Ct. R. 11, 22.

50. *Cf.* Sup. Ct. R. 43.

51. Sup. Ct. R. 45.

52. Sup. Ct. R. 44.

53. Sup. Ct. R. 44(1).

54. Based on Table IV(c), The Supreme Court, 1951 Term, 74 Harv. L. Rev. 97, at 105 (1960).

55. For example, the school-segregation decision, Brown v. Board of Educ., 347 U.S. 483 (1954).

56. Hart, *supra* note 17, at 91.

57. Hughes, The Supreme Court of the United States 67 (1936).

58. Hart, *supra* note 17, at 93.

59. London, The World of Law, 2 Vol. (1960).

60. Hart, *supra* note 17, at 93.

61. Dick v. New York Life Ins. Co. 359 U.S. 437, 458, 459 (1959).

62. *Cf.* Hart, *supra* note 17, at 96.

63. Douglas, The Supreme Court and Its Case Load, 45 Cornell L. Q. 401, 411 (1960).

64. Sup. Ct. R. 58.

65. Quoted in Hughes, *supra* note 57, at 71.

66. The story is recounted in Hughes, *supra* note 57, at 73.

67. Sup. Ct. R. 58(4).

68. For a description of the litigation which followed Brown v. Board of Educ., 347 U.S. 483 (1954), see McKay, With All Deliberate Speed, 43 Va. L. Rev. 1205 (1957). Such litigation is still continuing in Virginia, Louisiana, and elsewhere.

69. 304 U.S. 64.

70. Black and White Taxi Co. v. Brown and Yellow Taxi Co. 276 U.S. 518.

71. Swift v. Tyson 41 U.S. (16 Pet.) 1.

72. 367 U.S. 643.

73. 338 U.S. 25.

Chapter 6

1. Scotland and Northern Ireland have their own separate judicial systems, although appeals lie to the House of Lords. As for Commonwealth nations, their appeals, if heard by any English court, go to the Privy Council.

2. The only exceptions are (1) rare cases which may come before the court under the Fugitive Offenders Act, 1881, or (2) contempt of court cases.

3. Jackson, The Machinery of Justice in England 23 (3rd ed., 1960).

4. *Id.* at 25–26.

5. *Id.* at 27–29.

6. *Id.* at 65.

7. *Id.* at 80.

8. The Lord Chancellor is also a member, but in practice he does not sit.

9. Jackson, *supra* note 3, at 34, 95.

10. *Id.* at 50–53.

11. *Id.* at 65.

12. *Id.* at 79.

13. *Id.* at 79.

14. *Id.* at 238.

15. Supreme Court of Judicature (Consolidation) Act, 1925, ch. 49 § 9.

16. The Judges Remuneration Act, 1954.

17. The number of cases heard in 1961 (the first year of four divisions) was 617, as against 515 and 412 in 1960 and 1959, respectively.

18. Jackson, *supra* note 3, at 79.

19. The old Law Revision Committee did not have this advantage.

20. Evershed, The Judicial Process in Twentieth Century England, 61 Colum. L. Rev. 761 (1961).

21. Rules of Supreme Court (Appeals), 1955 O. 58, R. 3, § 2.

22. Rules of Supreme Court (Appeals), 1955 O. 58, R. 3, § 3.

23. Rules of Supreme Court (Appeals), 1955 O. 58, R. 5.

24. *Ibid.*, R. 6.

25. Rules of Supreme Court (Appeals), 1955 O. 58, R. 5, 11.

26. *Id.*

27. *Ibid.*, R. 11, note.

Chapter 7

1. Jackson, The Machinery of Justice in England 109 (3rd ed., 1960).

2. *Id.* at 97.

3. *Ibid.*

4. Williams, The Administration of Justice Act, 1960, 1961 Crim. L. Rev. 87; Devlin, Statutory Offences, 4 J. Soc. P.T.L. (n.s.) 206.

5. Goddard, Organization and Jurisdiction of the Courts of England, 44 J. Am. Jud. Soc'y (1960).

6. Jackson, *supra* note 1, at 231 et seq.

7. *Id.* at 109.

8. *Ibid.*

9. *Ibid.*

10. Rex v. Taylor (1949) 2 K.B. 368; Stone, Stare Decisis, 14 M.L.R. 219. The Criminal Law Revision Committee, appointed by the Home Secretary, occupies a position in criminal law roughly equivalent to that occupied in civil law by the Law Reform Committee.

11. Criminal Appeal Act (1907) § 4.

12. *Ibid.*

13. Goddard, The Working of the Court of Criminal Appeal, 2 J. Soc. P.T.L. (n.s.) 1.

14. Criminal Appeal Act (1907) § 17.

15. *Id.* at § 9.

16. Criminal Appeal Act (1907) § 19.

Chapter 8

1. Jackson, The Machinery of Justice in England 80 (3rd ed., 1960); Administration of Justice (Appeals) Act, 1934, 24 & 25 Geo. 5 c. 40, 18 Halsbury's Statutes 523.

2. Jackson, *supra* note 1, at 83. The Privy Council also has jurisdiction over some domestic matters not of present concern.

3. The Appellate Jurisdiction Act, 1876, 39 & 40 Vict. c. 59 § 3, 1876; 5 Halsbury's Statutes 293.

4. Cf. Jackson, *supra* note 1, at 111–12.

5. Administration of Justice Act, 1960 (8 & 9 Eliz. 2 c. 65) (1960). Appeals also lie from a Divisional Court of the Queen's Bench Division and from the Courts-Martial Appeal Court, in which cases those courts must grant leave to appeal. An exception is in habeas corpus cases, where appeal lies from a Divisional Court of the Queen's Bench Division without leave. Administration of Justice Act, 1960, § 15.

6. Jackson, *supra* note 1, at 84.

7. *Id.* at 80.

8. The Privy Counsellors who are qualified are those who hold or have held high judicial office within the meaning of the Appellate Jurisdiction Acts, 1876 and 1887. The judges overseas are qualified by virtue of the Judicial Committee Amendment Act, 1895, as amended by the Appellate Jurisdiction Acts, 1908 and 1913, and the Administration of Justice Act, 1928.

9. Jackson, *supra* note 1, at 376–77.

10. Jackson, *supra* note 1, at 83.

11. Denning, From Precedent to Precedent (Romanes Lecture, 1959, Oxford. Clarendon Press).

12. Landau, Precedents in the House of Lords, 63 Jurid. Rev. 232 (1952).

Chapter 10

1. See Chapters 7 and 9.

2. 45 J. Am. Jud. Soc'y 254–55 (1962).

3. *Id.*

4. *Id.*

5. *Id.*

6. See Chapter 6.

7. See Chapter 7.

8. See Chapter 8.

9. See Chapter 7.

10. See Chapter 5.

11. See Chapter 8.

12. See Chapter 7.

13. See Chapters 6 and 9.

14. But see Chapter 4.

15. Internal Operating Procedures of Appellate Courts, A Report by a Committee of the Section of Judicial Administration of the American Bar Association (1961), p. 47 et seq.

16. See Chapter 6.

17. *Id.*

18. See Chapter 7.

19. Brown v. Board of Education, 347 U.S. 483 (1954). See also Chapter 5.

20. Baker v. Carr, 82 Sup. Ct. 691 (1962).

21. Engel v. Vitale, 82 Sup. Ct. 1261 (1962).

INDEX